Myths of Magical Native American Women

Other books by Teresa Pijoan from Sunstone Press

American Indian Creation Myths
Dead Kachina Man
Granger's Threat
Healers on the Mountain
Native American Creation Stories of Family and Friendship
Pueblo Indian Wisdom
Ways of Indian Magic

Myths of Magical Native American Women

Including

Salt Woman Stories

by

Teresa Pijoan, PhD

SUNSTONE PRESS

SANTA FE

Photographs by Claire M. Connally and Nicole D. Garling.

Except where actual historical events and characters are being described for the story lines within this book, all situations in this publication are fictitious and any resemblance to living persons is purely coincidental.

Sunstone books may be purchased for educational, business, or sales promotional use. For information please write: Special Markets Department, Sunstone Press, P.O. Box 2321, Santa Fe, New Mexico 87504-2321.

Book and cover design › L. Ahl
Printed on acid-free paper
∞
eBook 978-1-61139-568-6

Library of Congress Cataloging-in-Publication Data
Names: Pijoan, Teresa, 1951- author.
Title: Myths of magical Native American women : including Salt Woman stories
  / by Teresa Pijoan, PhD.
Description: Santa Fe : Published by Sunstone Press, [2018] |
Identifiers: LCCN 2018048754 (print) | LCCN 2018054346 (ebook) | ISBN
  9781611395686 () | ISBN 9781632932495 (softcover : alk. paper)
Subjects: LCSH: Indian mythology–North America. | Indians of North
  America–Folklore. | Indian women in literature.
Classification: LCC E98.F6 (ebook) | LCC E98.F6 P525 2018 (print) | DDC
  398.2089/97–dc23
LC record available at https://lccn.loc.gov/2018048754

WWW.SUNSTONEPRESS.COM
SUNSTONE PRESS / POST OFFICE BOX 2321 / SANTA FE, NM 87504-2321 /USA
(505) 988-4418 / ORDERS ONLY (800) 243-5644 / FAX (505) 988-1025

Dedication to magical women:

My God Mother – Alice Marriott
My Mentor – Bertha Dutton
My Soul Sisters – Millie De Fabio, Carolyn Herem and Usha Prabhune
My Spiritual Aunt – Carol Honvantewa
My Daughters – Nicole Diane Garling and Claire Marie Connally
My Granddaughter – Lillian Mae Connally

And, of course, to the Special Man who makes life possible:
Thomas Edward Van Etten

Contents

Preface

The stories within this book are about high-spirited women who lived a self-controlled life, dealing within complex cultures. Storytelling cultures hold tightly to their history, beliefs and vulnerability. There is the universe, which is multilayered. The people are always referred to as First People, regardless of being the Second, Third People or Fourth People. Spirit Beings allow Humankind to breathe and to live in a world where there is order and consequence. The Clouds, Winds, Birds and Holy Places are Alive and watching. Spirit Beings make up the air, sky, and universe, existing in all things surrounding humankind.

There is a mental ability of an order, which brings a higher level of intelligence and awareness, coming from living with nature and breathing in control of self. Each culture uses symbolism to represent the four directions of North, East, West and South (NEWS). Also, there is an awareness of horizontal plains of consciousness. Native People know there are at least six different plains of consciousness, not all are here on this earth or in this place. Spirit beings are to be respected for out of this respect comes the ability to enhance one's life either through purpose or reward. Those who remember the stories of the Old Ones who have instructed, as teachers, the concepts of the universe on how it is run, the rules and its essence, will survive. Great rituals are taught with legendary knowledge the greatness of the supernatural who creates, manages and brings about working life.

The actions in the stories are important, not the words. Plants die, rivers run dry, animals disappear. Renewal comes from ceremonies done by humankind to recharge or readjust humankind's actions thus bringing the full potential to be in harmony with Nature. Activity can change the whole operation of existence, either good or bad. Humankind's energy is limited when used alone, only by working with the supernatural can humankind continue to exist in Nature.

Native American attitude toward sex is different in each culture. Many nomadic groups view women as caretakers of the children, the elderly and the main camp while the men go out to hunt or work. This leaves the women to remember much of the histories, since men are expendable and disappear at times. Matrilineal families are vital for the grandmothers hold the power and the mothers are taught how to use it in healing, childrearing, gathering, cooking and remembering.

Pueblo people, who are more sedentary, have matrilineal strengths as well. Uncles, the brothers of the mother, teach the children the ways of her people and her family. They are the mainframe of most families who travel back and forth to the uncles' home to learn. Thus, fathers teach their sisters' children. Grandmothers and Grandfathers are the Holders of the oral histories and traditional stories.

Many of the older traditional families speak of a time when once a child was born, there was a period of celibacy for seven years. The full attention was given to this child to learn, participate in ceremony and become responsible and honorable to their parents and grandparents. As modernization came into their lives, this changed.

Magical women stories are all about women who are to accomplish a powerful goal. Some of these women have parental guidance, most do not. It is known that women receive their power from Earth Mother when Father Sky is sleeping. Men receive their power from Father Sky, during the daytime. Women use the power of the Earth to bring strength, wisdom and knowledge. Salt Woman stories were almost lost. Once called to hear Grandpa Raymond's Salt Woman story, there was a need to find others to confirm her existence. More Salt Woman stories arrived through passive conversation and reaching out to the Elders. Evidently, Salt Woman existed all throughout the United States and into Canada and down south to Guiana. Problems came about when only partial memories of Salt Woman's travels arose. Only full stories are within these pages.

Amazingly two of the stories here were told by people younger than fifty years of age. They remembered their grandparents' tellings every fall when the cranes would fly south and the nights became cold. Sitting around the cooking fire, roasting corn for fall dances, the story of her was shared. Salt Woman definitely had a difficult existence as a spiritual being. She was tested, abused and she worked with great difficulty to give her gift to humankind. She survives to this day and continues to be generous.

Other magical women, in this book, are equally mysterious and powerful. There are many more stories of magical women that have been lost or only partially remembered. These are still being researched for a later publication. Women work with healing, regeneration and power. They exist in harmony with the male germinator who is the pollinator of life, a strong protector and provider.

Please enjoy these stories. Please pass them on to others for stories are meant to be kept alive. Share your stories, for your history is important and certainly worthy of being remembered.

–Teresa Pijoan, PhD
Goat Farm, New Mexico

1   Salt Bush and Ma'We Story
(Zuni)

Salt Bush is readily available in the Southwest. The dried root and blossoms are ground separately and the two powders combined. Moistened with saliva, this mixture is used externally to cure ant bites. When moistened with saliva or river water, if the powder is not available, the fresh blossoms are bruised then applied directly to an insect bite. This poultice keeps the swelling localized and the sting from hurting. Kemawe is also known as salt weed. Prayer plumes are attached to twigs of this plant and sacrificed to the cottontail rabbit at the winter solstice with prayers. This ceremony brings rabbits during the cold hunting season.

Fat, fluffy clouds of opal white rolled across the Rocky Mountain cliffs of red and purplish brown, making luminous shadows through the changing sun. The canyons, narrow and deep fall into darkness. The sun fought to reach through the blanket of white clouds to glow on the great mesas covered with fine sand. The contrast of sparkling silicate dust and mixed caliche illuminated the mountains of blue to deep vermilion.

"My daughter, it is time we spoke of your purpose here in the Cloud People's village. Please come and sit with us in the circle." White hair flowed around the hardened face of an older woman with eyes of sky blue. The ancient woman's skin was white as dried parchment. She beckoned the young woman with her long fingers bent and gnarled, pointing to a space in the circle of Spirit People. It was not something anyone would wish, to sit in the Circle of Judgment. Ageless entities sat with their legs tucked under them. White and grey floated around each. The young woman cautiously entered into the empty space on the cloud, which was turning from white to a deep bluish thundercloud.

Bowing her head to the elders, she tried to maintain an even breath. Her dark blonde hair floated around her head with the dancing winds. Kneeling, with her feet under her, she placed her hands on her lap, still not lifting her head, waiting for the verdict. Words from the Spirit to her mother's right spoke first, "Young one, you are not of our people. You have color to your face, your eyes are of a blue-green. Your hair is the color of the earth below. No, you are not of us."

The next Spirit kept their voice low, "Young one, you have a gender to you. It is obvious that you are a woman, part of the earth."

The young woman closed her eyes. Tears fell down her cheeks onto her lap. She knew this day would come. This day of rejection. How could she fight this? How could she change who she is? This was not her doing. Her mother was the one who went to earth and came back with earth inside of her. Slowly, she raised her head.

"The way of the Cloud People is to bring Sky Pollen to the earth. This I know. The way to unfold the mountain clouds for early awakenings, I know. The language of the Cloud People is known to me. Each one of you is loved by me, this you know."

She wanted to pull their awareness of sameness out of them. "What made me is unknown to me. Where I originated, is unknown to me. How is it right to send me to a place that I do not know? Who can I be? When 'One' of you is who I am?"

Elder Mother lifted her hand. Long fingers reached across the circle to the young woman. Caressing her daughter's fingers, she whispered, "You are not to be blamed for who or what you are. This is not the purpose of this circle. We wish to send you to do good things on the earth. You shall have a gift to give to the Earth People. This gift is important and something you can do, which we cannot." Her long fingers continued to stroke the young woman's hand.

Sky Spirit Watcher spoke next, "Yes, you are different. We have known you are different since you were born. Your mother was punished with the curse of gender. As you know, we are all hermaphrodites. We chose to be neither male nor female, but to be both. This way rain is made. It comes from both the female who is the giver of life and the male who is the pollinator of life. You are incomplete to be with the Cloud Spirits."

She nodded her head. Yes, she was made to be precisely a woman. She could not make rain by herself. Closing her eyes, again, she whispered, "What is it that I am to do?"

Thunder Holder's voice roared with pride, "We shall send you with the gift of salt. The Earth People have no knowledge of how to preserve or flavor food. They work hard with the hunt yet their food spoils within weeks. They will die if they cannot hunt and keep jerky in the cold of winter with the deep snows."

"Salt?" She turned to study Thunder Holder. Lightning Keeper clapped his hands, causing sparks to fly around his head. "Yes, now you are a Spirit, but once on earth you shall be made of salt. You shall give this gift to the Earth People. You shall show them how to use it in their food. You shall be an Earth-Spirit Salt Woman." Rubbing his hands together, the sparks were contained.

Flying Wind flew around her head, "Yes, it is time for you to have your place. You shall be cared for and loved by the Earth People for your gift." Flying Wind then slowed to add, "Sadly once you are on earth, you will not be able to return. That is the way of the purpose."

Grumbling in unison, the Spirit Clouds rolled away from her to disappear. Sitting alone, the young woman wrapped her arms around herself. The wind blew around her body wildly. Drops of white rain fell on her. A thin white manta appeared on her body. She put out her arms to let it wrap closed. Rain fell hard, burning her skin as she fell through the clouds, down, down, down onto the soft sand near flowing silver water.

Opening her eyes, she stared at the vast expanse of land. High over her were black ravens, a pair of them, floating on the wind currents. Mountains crusted with black lava and white gypsum framed the flowing river. Everything was huge and overwhelming. Her mincing steps took her to the edge of the glistening liquid, rippling over rocks and fallen tree branches. Blinking at Sun's bright reflection in the water, she put her hand out to capture the rays. Frightened she stepped back, her hand appeared dark as it blocked the Sun. "There is much to learn." Her words were drowned out by the sound of the pulsing river.

Turning her head, she noticed brush, grasses, small trees and plants with spines around her bare feet. Behind her on the ground, she noticed white powder filled each indentation of her footsteps. The white manta dress felt scratchy against her skin. Rubbing her hands along her arms, white powder fell floating around her, then to the dirt. Reaching up to the sky, she studied a large white cloud hovering above. "Help! Help me, please!" The cloud slowly drifted to the north, changing shape only to leave her alone.

This young woman was slender, appearing frail. Her white manta swung with her short, calculated steps. It was ankle-length, above her white fragile feet. The white cloth reflected the sunlight, glowing in contrast with the faded brown dirt surrounding her. Her feet felt the wisps of grass. She remembered her mother's words, "Life flows together with all the others, complete to one another, merged in one moment of sharing."

Earth People would complete her task. They were known to her. Drumming and song had brought the Cloud People to the Earth People. Closing her eyes, she remembered the people dancing. Elderly grandfathers hunched over with brushed moccasins, gray hair braided, thoughts of only rain and fertility for the land. Small children barely able to walk, carrying pine boughs with bells wrapped around their ankles searching the Sky for Rain. Humble women in beautiful mantas, bleached from the Sun, woven fine with the colors of the earth embroidered on the hem. The soft brown eyes searched, begged for the Cloud People to come and bring Yep-nan-ne, Sky pollen to the crops, the land and the children. She remembered them.

Sun moved across the earth eager to fall into His bed for the night. Watching for Cloud Color, she clapped in joy when the clouds turned from light pink to dark red and then glowed golden as Sun fell into his bedroll. Dark blue-black fell around her and she felt vulnerable. Searching for a safe place to rest, the chipmunks and squirrels chirped around her, pulling her interest to them and into a safe grassy place to repose. Closing her eyes, she slept soundly, dreaming of her soft bed high above, a fluffy cloud filled with warmth and those she loved surrounding her.

Rolling thunder awakened her as the Sun lifted from the golden pink plateau on the mesa to her right. A strange sensation entered, she was hungry.

Wind shook a tree above her arroyo bed. Bristly brown cones of wood pummeled down on her head. Sappy substance made some of the cones stick in her hair, on her manta, on her hand. They were too hard to eat. She studied the strange projectiles with hard leafy compartments enclosed in brown goo.

She tossed one against a boulder after she tried to lick it. Quick as a flash, a squirrel grabbed the cylindrical cone. Tearing open each compartment, there was a nut. He offered it to Salt Woman. She stared.

Squirrel placed the nut in his mouth, with his front teeth he cracked the outer shell. Spitting out the soft middle, he offered it to Salt Woman. Trusting him, she put the pithy fruit in her mouth. "Yum, this is good. Let me try?"

Squirrel studied the pine cones around her. Salt Woman picked one to follow Squirrel's example. Once she conquered several of the pine nuts, Squirrel placed a nut into the palm of her hand. He rolled the pine nut firmly tickling her fingers. The white powder covered the pine nut, Squirrel ate it. His fluffy red tail jerked back and forth. His large cheeks pulled back to reveal a smile.

Smiling, she asked, "Ah, it is better with salt, right?"

Squirrel squeaked to run down the far side of the boulder and disappear. Slowly, she learned the ways of the Earth. Rabbits, chipmunks, other squirrels and coyotes helped her on her path. After many Sunny days and Moon lit nights, Salt Woman realized the hollow feeling of being completely alone. No Earth People came to her nor did she find them. Several times she heard a drumming, similar to the Sky Thunder, but when she arrived, no one was there.

Salt Woman walked out of an arroyo. Patches of shell, dead animal skins, and ribbons of grass had repaired her manta. Her bare feet had blisters on the soles and sides of each foot. She appeared to be covered in dirt that sparkled in the full sun and floated from her body when the wind blew. Blue- green eyes searched the land for food, water, or shelter. Dark blonde hair floated around her body with each trying step of movement. Long fingers pushed aside the loose hair from her field of vision, only to grasp the air in front of her as if to pull her body forward. Slowly as her body rose from the arroyo, there appeared behind her a small child.

The child was thin. Dark hair covered his ethereal face and shoulders. His feet staggered with each attempt to follow the adult ahead. A voice cried out, a boy's voice called for the woman in front to stop, to wait, to listen. "You are Salt Woman! I am your Spirit. Wait for me!" The woman did not, but continued in her quest.

"Stop! Stop! I'm hungry and I'm thirsty! Stop!" Neither stopped, but moved forward with wind billowing sand around them and Sun beating down heat. The boy's feet were wrapped with dark moccasins and his kilt that once had been bleached white by the Sun was now brown from dirt. Hands moved forward to grab at the woman. She was far, too far ahead of him to be reached.

Suddenly, the woman stopped. Her manta flowed about her ankles, her long hair floated around her, but her eyes peered with stern awareness and her head was tilted to listen. "Water, there is water nearby. Come, let's find it. Life flows together with all the others, complete to one another, merged in one moment of sharing."

Twisting, she took hold of his wrist in her filthy hand and pulled him along beside her. They both picked a stronger pace, lurching toward the east. The sound of rushing water became louder. She dropped his wrist and ran. The boy quickly overtook her to reach the flowing waters of the Rio Grande. He did not stop, but fell full face into the cool water. Laughing as the water pulsed over him, he cried out, "I may be your spirit, but this is my dear friend!" He cupped his hand to spray Salt Woman with the wet substance.

Standing ankle deep, Salt Woman noticed some of the water moved around her legs, while much of the water was absorbed around her white skin. The weight of the water hurt her. Slowly, backing up and out of the water, she noticed as the water filled her empty footsteps, the water turned white and hot. The burning liquid scorched her toes. Salt Woman turned to run to dry land. The boy continued to giggle, roll and play in the silvery fluid that engulfed his small body.

"Salt Woman, do not stand still! Run, run to me and then lie flat on your back. Run! Come on! Run to me!" The boy called to her while attempting to stand, "Your mother sent me to help you find people. The hard crust of your salt has not been removed, we can play in the water! Come on, run to me!"

The young woman took a deep breath, holding her arms out by her side, she raced to the boy. Her feet moved across the water without entering. She could feel the water on the bottoms of her feet, but not on her ankles or calves. Momentum and the force of freedom, allowed her to flow over the water directly to the young boy. He put his arms out to her and they both fell into the water.

The rushing river gushed over them and their clothes. They bobbed downstream, letting the water propel them over rocks, down shallow water-falls, to the easy surface of sand near a Pueblo. Salt Woman laughed as she struggled to her feet. She shook her head, letting the droplets of water fling from her long hair. The manta now whiter, appeared to not contain any water at all. Bending gracefully, she lifted the boy by his arms to stand. His eyes sparkled. His woven kilt clung to his body and his thin legs. The moccasins were balloons of water around his small feet.

The woman whispered to him, "Listen, do you hear that?"

Turning toward the south, the boy smiled, "Sniff the air, do you smell what I smell?"

Taking his hands in hers, she flung him around her. Water, sand, and laughter flowed about them in a circle. Setting him on the ground, she pointed south, "Let's go find some food and perhaps some shelter." They walked faster. Salt Woman combed her long hair with her thin fingers. The boy pulled a piece of yarn from his kilt. He wrapped his hair around his wrist and with the white yarn he tied his hair into a chongo. Sun dried their bodies.

Drums beat loudly in the plaza. Dancers pounded the ground with their feet. Hornos hot with baking bread stood behind the cooking fires. Pots hung heavy over the fire flame with pasole stew bubbling near the kiva. Children ran around the adults, playing. Adults who weren't dancing, stood watching family dancers, nodding in appreciation. The heartbeat from the drums was changed to a fast tempo as those who had danced since dawn left the plaza in single file and new dancers arrived from the eastern side of the plaza. Dancers ranged in age from great-grandparents to little toddlers, all anxious to show their respect to the Spirits through dance.

Salt Woman was aware of the testings in being accepted by the Earth People. Becoming one of them, settling down, and adapting, of giving up part of herself would be difficult. She was ready for she was Salt Woman. Turning to take the boy's hand for confidence, he was gone. Hurrying to reach the center of the village to catch him, she noticed the sentinels standing on the roofs of the houses. Studying the sky quickly, she saw clouds hovering in the west, watching her. Taking a deep breath, she rubbed her manta with her hands to walk into the village.

Salt Woman found the boy on a sandy hill, standing, watching the other children who were playing in a spring. Older children were getting their kilts and mantas arranged by family to be ready to dance. Salt Woman and the boy quietly slipped into the audience to watch the dancers. The boy studied the people more than the dance. He tightly held the woman's hand and tried to hide behind her white manta. People ignored him. Everyone watched until the sun started to slide down the western horizon. Tables were brought outside along with handmade tree trunk benches. Drums became quiet, the dancers departed, and the families moved to the tables ready for nourishment.

Salt Woman turned to join in the slow change from plaza to food tables. Families were talking, laughing, sharing stories of past dances and she quietly took a wooden bowl and with a ceramic spoon filled the bowl full of food. Smiling at the people who met her, and nodding to the children, she folded a loaf of bread into her manta skirt. When she felt the bread was well hidden, she filled her wooden bowl with what she found delicious.

Three loaves disappeared within the folds of her manta dress, bowl after bowl was filled to nourish their starving bodies. People ignored them as much as they themselves were ignored. Night fires were lit, songs began with soft drumming, and children quietly slept on woven blankets at their families' feet. In the corner of the plaza, under an old tree, Salt Woman found the boy sleeping. She put his head in her lap. He softly slept while she took in the warmth of those around her. Now, the boy was content. She turned at the sound of laughing women's voices.

Gently letting the boy sleep on the soft ground, Salt Woman rose to follow the women who were putting the extra food away in bundles of cloth or in carrying pottery bowls. Women spoke quietly as they worked, not noticing her presence. Suddenly, they stopped. Salt Woman put her hand on one of the grandmother's arms. The grandmother jerked her arm away, "What is it that you want? What are you doing here? You're not one of us."

Salt Woman shook her head, her blue-green eyes glowed with kindness. "No, we came for the feast. The dancing was beautiful and the food was good. If you would like, I could make the food even better. I can make the food last longer and bring a stronger flavor. Would you like me to do this?"

The women backed away from her. Some were hugging the loaves of bread. The grandmother studied the strange woman. Looking her up and down, she asked, "How would you do this? Are you a spirit? Are you trying to take our food? What do you want?"

Salt Woman lifted a sharp knife from the table. Then pulled up her manta. Reaching further on the table, she picked a wooden bowl. Slowly, carefully, she scraped the inside of her thigh to let white powder fall into the bowl. One woman screamed, the others grabbed what they could and ran from her. The one grandmother stood strong to watch. "What are you doing?"

Salt Woman put the bowl on the table and beside it the knife. "This is a gift that I give to you out of gratitude for the good food and the dancing. If you mix this into your food, it will last longer and the taste will be richer." The grandmother took the bowl from her hand only to dump the contents onto the ground. "Get out of our pueblo! Don't come back. Get your boy and go." She dropped the bowl on the ground upside down.

The soft night breeze blew the white powder into dark. Slowly, Salt Woman walked to the sleeping boy. Gracefully lifting him by his upper arms, she stood him upright. "It is time for us to leave." Rubbing his eyes, he did not question this, but only followed her out onto the flat dry desert night. An arroyo was found, a small cave niche was dug and the two of them slept intertwined until dawn. The awareness that she knew little of life and less of her purpose penetrated painfully to an ultimate truth. Earth People were not accepting of her.

The loaves of bread kept them fed for four days. At dusk, they heard the coyotes following them, but never did they come close.

The summer sun was hot. The flat desert was dry. Rarely did they find water. Deciding to stay far away from other pueblos, since the news of their travels would have moved quickly after the last feast day dance, Salt Woman aged in the heat. Her youthful face wrinkled and cracked. The boy appeared to become thinner and weaker as he walked.

Twice they found the Rio Grande again, four times they attempted to enter pueblos hearing feast day dances. The last two gave them food and even shelter, but they did not want anything of hers and this was made clear. Not wanting to overstay their visit and or hospitality of others, they moved on further south each day, each night, with hope of finding their place to belong. White cranes flew overhead trying to push them toward Laguna Pueblo. Salt Woman shied away from the sound of the drums for fear they would hurt her or the boy.

The last pueblo they came to was Zuni. Dancers were there from many of the other pueblos. Salt Woman noticed the people arriving, camping outside of the village and knowing they needed food desperately, she attempted to enter. No one appeared to recognize her or the boy. The woman moved among the crowds of people, watching the dances, taking food, listening to the talk. Until she met someone who remembered her well.

The grandmother stood firmly in front of the woman. "Do you remember me? Do you remember when you gave me the bowl?" The grandmother's words were not harsh, but kind. "I found some of the white powder and used it in my bread dough. It was just to try, but everyone wanted my bread after that. Some of the white powder was put into my stew and my family could not get enough of it. You were right, the food lasts longer and it tastes better."

Salt Woman looked down and did not reply. The grandmother took the woman's cracked dry hands and rubbed them. "You need some animal fat for these fingers. Come with me, bring the boy." They went into a make shift lean-to. The grandmother rubbed their fingers and faces with animal fat. Afterwards, she fed them bread and stew. Humming softly, she guided them to a blanket where they could rest. "You are welcome here. Many of the others have been told of your ways and your struggles. Some of our runners were watching out for you as you travelled. This is my sister's pueblo and you are safe here."

The two slept through the night. They were content. When the dawn light awakened the people, the two strangers were gone. The people tried to follow the footprints in the dirt, but they went in different directions. The boy's footprints went to the west up Mount Taylor. After a time, they disappeared as if he was lifted into the sky. The woman's footprints went to the south, ending at the lake. When they people tried to drink the water, it was too salty to quench a thirst. Some of the people slept that night at the edge of the lake.

In the morning, they all spoke of the same dream. The woman was known as Salt Old Woman and because of her unrest with people, she had chosen to live in the lake. If the people needed or wanted salt, they could come to the lake and retrieve it, but there was a ceremony of respect that was needed. A man could gather the salt, but only after fasting and giving respect to her. Salt could only be harvested in the fall and the spring, not in the heat of summer or the cold of winter. People come from many different pueblos to Zuni Salt Lake to harvest salt.

2 Salt Old Woman (Tanoan)

Near Chamita, New Mexico, there is a place where the rivers converge. The waters from two different worlds come together to become one river of Great Power. This one river is known as the Rio Grande, the Big River. Here right before the birth of this one river is a small island. Each river is separated by this island and few were able to wade the mighty current to arrive there. Here is where some of the Old Ones say the birth of the Salt Woman happened.

The spring runoff from the gorge was magnificent. Fish were jumping, leaping up into the air to avoid being dashed on the rocks under the water. Ducks flew crazily around, grabbing the flying good in a frenzy. Heron, geese, long necked cranes flocked to this island for the bounty. Harsh winds ripped away at the bare cottonwood tree branches, flinging them into the water. The night air had a cold sting to it as temperatures dropped below freezing. Many remember this spring as a strange time.

The hunters had to move higher into the mountains to find game, even though the land was still covered with snow and ice. The natural salt cedar and sweet grass struggled to survive and the fall would bring a sad harvest of ground meal. The terraced gardens planted with carefully placed seedlings were washed out with torrential downpours and eroding foothills. Babies cried throughout the night and the elderly groaned with sore aching joints.

Finally, northern rains abated. The river waters stilled to gently flow. Birds flew high in the sky, winging their way northward. Herds of deer and wild elk cautiously wove their way down the mountains to the patches of sweet grass and billowing wheat. A quiet peace came upon the land. Elders shook their heads, all of this made them worry. Children ran playing in the center of the pueblos as mothers wove on looms and father's worked on rebuilding adobe homes.

From the island came a woman's song. The voice hovered on the breezes in the morning and haunted the evening stillness. No one knew who would be on the island and no one particularly wanted to explore. Then one morning, the song's location moved. As mothers stretched while rising from their pallets and fathers walked down to the river for water, they heard the song coming from high above them. Few wanted to go to the top of the mountain that protected them from the northern elements because there were mountain lions there, bobcats, and strange animals no one wanted to meet.

The people ignored the singing until one afternoon a young boy raced into the pueblo calling people to him. When he finally caught his breath, he said, "There is a young woman high in the wash. At first I thought she was a wild animal, covered in dirty leaves with branches in her hair and her dress is black with soot and clumps of mud. Her voice is the one we hear in the morning and evening." The young boy wiped his face with his hands, "One of the elders should go and see her."

The boy's mother grabbed him, "What were you doing up there? You were told not to go above the pueblo! What if she put a curse on you! Go home! You should have left her alone!" Others around the mother all clicked their tongues in agreement.

Later, when the Elders gathered it was decided. The oldest of the grandfathers who knew the land and knew the prayers of respect would go and meet with this woman. He would find her purpose and deal with her. Each Elder slowly went to their homes anxious for the meeting to be resolved. In the morning, four of the Elders went to the old grandfather's home to prepare him for the journey. When they called into the home, they were met with cries of sadness. The old man had died in his sleep.

The Elders stood outside, trying to decide what to do next. Fear had crept into them. If one of them was chosen would they die as well? Did this woman have this kind of power? The Elders were unsure in their course of action. They spoke, muttered, prayed, stood silent and watched the others around them. In the end, they chose to do nothing. They believed that sometimes it is best to wait and an answer will arise.

Spring gave way to summer and with the changing of the season, the temperature grew hot. Herds of wildlife moved into the canyon and disappeared. Birds no longer flocked around the river. The waters of the rivers became warmer with a loss of fish. Berries withered on the bush. The ground cracked from dryness and heat. Babies became sick with runny noses and bad coughs. Grandparents became stiff and unable to move. Parents and the youth fought and argued. Again, time was not good. Something had happened and now came the time to act.

Women gathered in the plaza as night fell. They spoke of the woman on the mountain. One older woman hushed them, "You have all been too busy to notice, but the woman is no longer there. She hasn't sung for us in many months. She must have moved to another place, perhaps to a place where the people were nicer to her." The others laughed, "No, no, she's still there. We shall go. We shall go and see her as women to woman. We can go in the morning!" It was agreed.

The early rising group of women met at the bottom of the arroyo. Some of the women had baskets coated with tree pitch, which were filled with water to share with the strange woman on the mountain. The women hiked to the top of the mountain, it took them all day. Once at the top, they saw no one, nothing, not a trace of a person ever being there. Some found lion paw prints and some smaller bobcat prints, but there was no person on their mountain.

She had moved to the south. Knowing the people of the pueblo knew of her and she knew they could hear her singing, she had migrated south. Her tattered black dress was at least cool in the high heat of the summer. Matted hair flowing down her back kept the holes in her dress from her skin to burning. Bare feet were blistered from the extreme temperatures of the caliche sand and rocky paths that she had to traverse. Dark brown eyes peered out at the world around her with many questions as to her purpose, her destiny and her place to belong.

When she walked across the flats below the mesas, her tracks were white. Sometimes when she chose a path across a dried marsh, water would gush out of her footprints to fill with white powder. She walked to the east, following arroyo after arroyo and gully after gully. Sleeping in a hollow tree or finding soft sand between two lava rocks was her only shelter. Coyotes and deer would sometimes follow her to lick the white powder left behind in her footsteps. After moving to the east and not finding anyone like her, she decided to follow the setting sun.

Visiting different pueblos; Oke Owingee, Santa Clara, San Ildefonso, Pojoaque, Nambe, Cuyumongue, Tesuque, Cochiti, Santo Domingo, San Felipe, she worked on mingling with the people. The people were kind enough to share their food, yet none of these pueblos wanted her to stay. After the food had been served and eaten, Salt Woman would pinch her nose with her thumb and forefinger and taking a deep breath in through her mouth, she would remove her fingers and blow mucous from her nose onto the remaining food. This white powder would cover the food.

Women grabbed their children to take them away. Quickly, the men carried her thin frail body to throw her out onto the hard dirt. No one wanted to have anything more to do with her. This happened over and over again, in one pueblo after another. Salt Woman continued to try and teach the people, but their disgust with her appeared to get in the way.

Quivira, Abo, Tenabo, Pecos River people, Isleta, Santo Domingo, Laguna, Acomita and finally Acoma—there were none who befriended her. Only the stars at night brought her peace. The sun shone down on her during the day, listening to her song and watching her as she moved from one place to another. Salt Woman became older, bent and slowly became weaker and less. Finally, she found her way to Black Mesa near Zuni.

The people there took pity on her. She did not speak their language, but from her appearance they knew she was in need. The woman in black was too weak to eat with others. This kept the others from knowing of her strange habit with food. Finally, the woman disappeared into the night. The Elders called for a vision of her, since she appeared to have great power. It was at this time they learned of her gift to them and where they could find it.

She is known as Old Salt Woman now living in a lake. She gives to the pueblos, but only when she is shown respect. Now, she has found her place. She is back in the water, separated from people and surrounded with wildlife and peace. Salt Old Woman found her home and to this day, she is still at Salt Lake at Zuni.

3   Salt Woman (Southeastern Creek)

Two Brothers lived with their grandmother in a chickee or a shelter constructed from logs with a steep roof. It was supported by posts, with a raised floor, a thatched roof, and open sides in the Big Cypress Swamp deep in the Ever Glades of Southern Florida. Grandmother kept the house and did the cooking for her grandsons who went out hunting every day. They were excellent hunters. They brought home birds and rabbits, eels and fish, and even big game such as deer and wild turkeys. They lived in a fine chickee. The holding posts were made of cypress poles, and the roof was thatched with palmetto.

Every spring, the young men gathered fresh palmetto fans and the Grandmother braided them into the old ones to make the roof thicker and tighter to keep out the rain. The floor was raised high above the ground to keep the Ever Glades' water outside. Floor rafters were close together, so there was room above them to store their seasonal goods. Off to the side of the large chickee was a smaller one where Grandmother stored dried food and had a cooking area. It was built with solid walls so no one could see into it. The brothers and Grandmother belonged to the Creek peoples (later known as Seminoles), who found the marshes and swamp areas safe from outsiders.

One morning, Grandmother watched her sons sharpen their spears and their arrows preparing for the hunt; the grandsons were just sitting there, sharpening their points. Grandmother called out to them, "Why aren't you out hunting? What's the matter?"

The younger grandson stared up at his grandmother, "We're tired of just eating meat! That's all we have to eat is meat. Certainly the Great Spirits didn't want us to live only off of meat."

The older grandson nodded in agreement, "The Great Spirits have made these beautiful animals. Each day we go out and kill them. There must be more to eat than the meat we hunt."

Grandmother smiled at her grandsons, "Go and hunt something fine for dinner. There will be surprise for you when you return."

The younger grandson shook his head, "The Great Spirits are truly great to give us such fine meat to live off of, but somehow the Great Spirits must have something else great for us to eat as well." He gathered his spears and put his arrows in his quiver. The two grandsons pulled their canoe from under the chickee and set off in search of meat.

Grandmother walked out to hand them some dried jerky. "When you return home today some of your dinner will already be cooked. What do you plan to bring home?"

The older grandson smiled warmly at his Grandmother, "Let's bring home deer for today will be a day to celebrate." They rowed off into the Ever Glades. All day they hunted. The brothers thought about what their grandmother had told them. The younger brother who was the curious one, said, "Do you think Grandmother can find us other food than meat?"

The older grandson reminded him, "Grandmother is very strong. She has powers and I believe she can use them."

Later in the evening, when the mists were rising from the bayous, the brothers looked up into the sky. They were surrounded with drooping ivy and branches dipping into the water, all they saw was the one lone star of evening. "Time to head home," the older brother said, pointing to the star. "We have had a good day's hunt." Animals swam in the water around them to cool from the heat of the day. Otters, manatees, alligators, and crocodiles silently dove and floated around their canoe. As they neared their chickee the brothers smelled a delicious odor. There was something cooking. There was a new smell coming from inside.

The youngest brother jumped out of the canoe, calling out, "Grandmother, Grandmother, what smells so good?"

Grandmother met him at the door of the chickee, "Go and butcher your deer to let it hang. I have already brought in some meat from the hanging shed. Once, you are done come to be excited about a new food." She wiped her hands on her cover cloth to smile at him. "You will have a new experience this evening for your meal."

The brothers carefully butchered the deer, hanging meat to dry. Washing their hands clean, they hurried into their Grandmother. Nodding to them, she stirred the large black pot with a long handled wooden spoon. Two brothers sat anxiously awaiting their delicious meal. Grandmother poured her concoction into two wooden bowls with two wooden spoons. The brothers stared at the stew, they had only had chunks of meat before, nothing as a soupy substance. Cautiously, they dipped in their spoons and tasted.

"Grandmother, this melts in my mouth. What are these yellow delicious round things?" The younger brother pointed to his spoon.

"Those are corn kernels." Grandmother smiled glad they enjoyed her meal.

"Where does corn come from, Grandmother?" The older brother licked his bowl.

"That is all I can tell you. If you liked the corn, then I shall cook with it again." Grandmother took their empty bowls back into the cooking chickee to wash. The brothers slept soundly that night.

In the morning, the brothers were busy sharpening their spears and collecting their bows and arrows. They were excited and talking quickly. Grandmother called out to them, "What are you going to hunt today?"

Older brother lifted his long spear, "Today, we go after wild turkeys. They will taste good with the corn!"

Grandmother clapped her hands together, "Tonight, I shall have something different for you! It would not be wise for you to become tired of eating corn."

Younger brother pulled out the canoe and off they rowed through the bayous. The brothers ducked under the live oak, wild lemon trees, and wild orange vines. Younger brother shook his head, "That corn was good, but I wonder what Grandmother will be cooking tonight?"

Older brother laughed, "Whatever it is it will be good. Grandmother is an excellent cook!"

Smiling, Younger brother added, "I don't think anything could be better than the corn!"

The turkeys were speared early in the evening. The brothers hurried back to the chickee for their new flavored dinner. As they got closer to the chickee, they smelled something different, but good. Grandmother took the turkeys, plucked the feathers, chopped up the meat to put in her large stew pot. The brothers knew better than to ask and waited patiently for their dinner.

Grandmother served them their wooden bowls of food. They tasted it. It tasted like corn, but didn't look like corn at all. "What is this?" Asked younger brother.

Grandmother studied him, "Don't you like it? Isn't it good?"

"Yes, yes, it is delicious. This has the taste of corn, but it isn't corn, what is it?"

"Its grits. Grits are a type of corn that is cooked differently. If you don't like it and would prefer something else, I will cook that tomorrow." Grandmother sat to watch them eat.

Older brother shook his head, "It's very good, we're not complaining, we just don't know where you get these delicious foods."

Grandmother collected their bowls, "I can't tell you. I can cook it for you, but I can't tell you where they come from." She went back into the chickee cooking hut.

The next day, the brothers walked across the small islands to hunt muskrats. When their hunting pouch was full, they returned home. Grandmother was already cooking in the chickee kitchen. The brothers called to her and gave her their pouch of muskrats. That evening they had muskrat stew with corn. The meal was filling and the brothers slept well again that night.

In the morning, the brothers gathered up their spears to hunt. Grandmother wished them well and went back into the large chickee to clean. The brothers walked away from the chickee until they came to an orange grove. The older brother went on ahead down the path. The younger brother hid in the orange grove to watch and find out where the corn came from. Younger brother hid crouched in the orange grove most of the day. The sweet smelling blossoms made him sleepy, but he stayed awake to watch. In mid-afternoon, Grandmother went into the cook chickee. She started the fire, put water in her cooking pot and then moved to the smaller storage chickee beside the kitchen chickee. The walls of the storage chickee were tightly closed logs. The logs were chinked with mud to keep out insects and rodents.

The roof was of looser thatch to let the heat from the storage room out and keep it cool.

Younger brother quietly climbed up the log wall to the roof. He lay silently on a bearing roof post and watched Grandmother. She took a treated deer skin and laid it on the floor. Then she took a wooden bowl and placed it on the dried skin. Carefully, she lifted up her skirt and with her palm she stroked the sides of her outer thigh. Corn kernels fell from her thigh into the bowl, some bounced out of the bowl and onto the skin. Grandmother did this until her bowl was filled. Then she dropped her skirt, lifted the bowl and put away the skin. Leaving the storage shed, she hurried to the cooking chickee.

Younger brother slid down the side of the storage shed wall. Quickly, he hurried down the path his brother had taken, to catch up with him. Older brother greeted him, "Where does Grandmother get the corn?"

Younger brother shook his head, "You are not going to believe this!"

"What? Where does she get the corn, tell me?"

Younger brother sat on a log and told his brother. Older brother stared at him, "No, that can't be right. Why would she think we would want to eat her? We wouldn't want to eat our Grandmother!"

Younger brother rubbed his eyes, "It is truth. That is what she did, I saw her with my own eyes."

Older brother sat on the log next to him, "Only Caddos and Tonkawas are people eaters. We would never eat anyone!"

"I don't want to eat my grandmother!" Younger brother stared out at the bayous.

When the brothers returned home empty handed, Grandmother simply clicked her tongue. "No problem, we have dried turkey jerky in the storage chickee. I will get it and add it to the stew."

The brothers could hardly swallow the food. It smelled good and they knew it was delicious, but they were disgusted at the thought of eating their grandmother.

Slowly, they tried please her, but they couldn't finish it.

Grandmother glared at them, "What is the problem? Don't you like my food? Why aren't you eating?"

The brothers looked at one another. The older brother said, "We are so tired of hunting that we can hardly chew or eat."

Grandmother grabbed their unfinished food bowls. "Go, just go! Aiee! I cannot believe you are so tired." Grandmother dropped the bowls, she threw up her arms and then collapsed on the floor planks.

The brothers were frightened. They knelt beside her, "What can we do to help you! What can we do?"

Younger brother lifted Grandmother's head into his lap. Looking up into his eyes, she said, "You have found out my secret now I must go way from you!"

Older brother knelt beside her, "Grandmother, we don't know anything except we need you. You can't leave us. How can we live without you? You are the wise one who teaches us and tells us about life! Please, you cannot leave us!"

Grandmother's face was now ashen gray, "You brothers are smart, you will learn much on your own. When I die, you must do exactly what I tell you to do now. Bury me in the field beside the bayou, put me in the field that does not flood with water. Lay my body in the earth and cover my body with rich dark soil. Build a fence of sticks from the flowering orange tree around my grave where I am buried. There will be large plant that will grow from where I am buried. It will grow tall, it will have tassels come out of the top of it, don't pick it, don't cut it, leave it be. The plant will grow tall, tall. Keep the wild hogs away from it, make sure the fence is strong and sturdy."

Grandmother took the hand of each brother, "In the spring, when the plant is very tall and has tassels, the plant will grow corn plants inside each leaf. Take the round, covered ears of corn into the storage shed. Do not eat them, they will be hard. Let them dry through the winter and then plant them again in the spring next to where I am buried. Keep the fence strong. In the fall, you will have a harvest of corn plants. Always dry some for planting in the spring. The others you can cook and eat. Do you understand?"

The Brothers both said, "Yes." They let their tears fall down on their grandmother. She closed her eyes. The Younger Brother then said, "What shall we do then, Grandmother?"

"You shall go out into the world and find yourselves wives. You both are of an age to have wives. Let the wives plant the hills of corn in the fenced area and let them cook for you. Always be kind and grateful to your wives for they shall work hard for you." Grandmother let her last breath leave her body.

Quietly, they carried Grandmother out to the field behind the bayou. They dug a deep pit with their wooden spades. As the evening approached, they slowly placed her in the pit and covered her with the rich dirt. Night fell, the brothers cut and fixed a sturdy fence around her grave site. That night, they went to bed sad and hungry. In the spring, they went out and found wives to bring home. In the fall, they harvested the corn as they had been instructed and both brothers lived a good life. Corn came to the Creek people and the Creek people learned to grow gardens.

4   Salt Woman vs Uncegila
(Eastern Lakota)

We were the herders of buffalo and the wild large animals. Our waters were good until there arrived a spirit that was a trickster and caused the water to go bad. Her name was Uncegila. She was large, round, and angry. First People did not recognize her as one of the First Women. Uncegila brought a thick silt to the waters. This made the water undrinkable. If the people did not say prayers to her or bring her sacred corn pollen she would flood the lands with silt water. She could bring up the silt from under the lakes and rivers, this made the land bad where nothing could grow.

At this time Salt Woman appeared to guide the people to large ponds where her salt lived. Salt Woman learned of Uncegila and how her anger was hurting First People. It wasn't easy to find Uncegila for she hid and if she knew someone was close to her, she would attempt to kill them. Salt Woman learned of where Uncegila was hiding from the coyotes and wolves. The animals smelt her stench. Cautiously camping near her, with the help of the animals, Salt Woman learned of songs that would appease Uncegila. Slowly, the two women met through songs and animals.

Salt Woman complimented Uncegila on her powerful voice and strong character. Uncegila, in turn, complimented Salt Woman on her tall stature. Thanking her, Salt Woman spoke of how healthy Uncegila was for no matter how much Salt Woman ate, she remained thin and pale.

Uncegila laughed, saying, "My round shape is not from eating, it is filled with the anger I feel for the First People."

Salt Woman shook her head, "Your anger is not good for you. How is it that your anger keeps you round?"

Uncegila agreed, "I asked the Spirits to fill me with evil. They keep putting all the evil there is inside of me. Soon, I shall unleash it on the First People. They do not accept me for who I am. It is not good to be arrogant or to be vain, but I should appreciate being known for who I am."

Salt Woman frowned, "You are known, for you have fouled the waters. You have brought sickness and death to many. First People know of you and they fear you."

"Yes, they should fear me. I was here when they arrived. I have been here since wind blew and grass grew." Uncegila pointed to the sweet grass on the plains. "These grasses will be taken from the First People."

Salt Woman nodded, "Sweet grass is important for survival. You have survived well here. First People don't know how to show you their appreciation."

Uncegila hit her fists against her thighs, "No, they don't. If they knew of the place on my body where they could kill me they would do so." Uncegila rubbed the muscle below her left shoulder above her breast. "This is the place where the Spirits forgot. This is the place where I am most human."

Salt Woman took Uncegila's hand, "Why are you determined to kill First People? Isn't there a way for them to be your friends?"

Uncegila jerked her hand away from Salt Woman, "No, they must die! They have no respect for what they don't understand."

"And you? Do you understand their fear of you?" Salt Woman stepped back from Uncegila, evil was oozing out of her mouth.

"No, I don't wish to understand them. They will die and be left as dust in their lack of respect."

Salt Woman studied Uncegila, "First People are young. They do not know the ways of the Spirits yet. It would be wise if we could both teach them."

Uncegila spit disgusting smelly saliva at Salt Woman, "They deserve to be dust and nothing more!" She turned away to go back to her hiding place.

Knowing this would not end well for First People, Salt Woman went to her sons who were The Twin War Gods. They were born from her Salt. The Twin War Gods had learned the ways of honor and respect. Salt Woman explained her conversation with Uncegila. They had a conference. It was decided the Twin War Gods would protect the First People. Sadly, Salt Woman told the Twin War Gods of the area where Uncegila was most vulnerable.

Uncegila dreamt a premonition of her death. Fearing this dream to come true, she chose to move away from the First People. Knowing water and filling it with silt, was her specialty. Moving to the east, she found the Moreau River. Soon the river was filled with silt. The buffalo would no longer come to drink from it. Searching for her, the Twin War Gods were told of this fouled lake. Now they knew this was her new home.

The Twins went after Uncegila. They dove into the waters down to where she lived. There they wrestled with her. Uncegila wrapped her body around one of the Twins and tried to squeeze him to death. The other Twin had great powers and held her head back until her mouth filled with foul silt. Gasping, she released her hold only to spit the smelling muck into one of the brother's eyes. He swam away from her. Using her long arms, she clutched onto his legs. Wrapping her fingers tightly around his thighs, his legs began to turn blue. Screaming in pain, he pulled a knife from his belt to cut her fingers off, letting them fall into the mud.

The other twin twisted her arm behind her to show the muscle below her shoulder. Kicking him hard in the chin, he fell back. Her free hand grabbed him around the neck, strangling him with all her might. Older Twin took his knife to stab her in the back. Letting go of the younger Twin's throat, she twisted to remove the knife. Swimming through the clouded mud, she went after the older Twin. This left her disoriented and confused for the fluid left her blinded. The Twin War Gods worked together to grab her around the waist. Her one working arm was held against her body. The older Twin took a sword from its sheath attached to his belt, to cut deeply into the muscle above her left breast.

Evil nasty pus squirted from her body. Quickly, they dragged her to the surface, pulling her onto the dry sand. Slowly, the smelly fluids gushed out of her as she became less and less. Finally, her head turned into sand. Winds swirled to disintegrate what was left, leaving only a slight imprint on the earth. The anger within Uncegila was let loose.

This dried area of silt and dried anger became the lands of Nebraska and the Badlands of the Dakota. This large desert, in the Americas, is thanks to Uncegila and the Twin War Gods. Salt Woman stopped the waters and lakes from having too much silt and once again the Buffalo could drink from good water. Lakota are grateful to Salt Woman and her sons. The waters of the lakes and rivers were safe, but now the newcomers have fouled the water and the Lakota sing, asking for Salt Woman to return with the Twin War Gods.

5 Ma'l Oyattsik-l or Salt Woman (Zuni)

Chamita or Ts'ama in Tewa is where the Rio Grande meets the Chama River. Chamita is the birth place of many spirits, good and bad. There was a time when the rains came, falling hard upon the land. Mud sloshed onto the banks and the water rose higher and higher. Rain once fell continuously until there was no more rain to fall. Mud and wet earth were everywhere. People moved to live high on the mountain mesas above the gorge near Taos. People were confused. Earth became a different color. She had shifted and the river was not where it once had been. Lowland homes and villages were nothing more but flattened dirt. Life changed.

Chamita, the birthplace of spirits now hardened. At any rate, out of this came a shape. Lying on the dried ground, there was movement. Dark, filthy and with a human shape arose a young woman. Her hair was the color of the earth. Her arms and legs were flakey, yellowish-white powder fell as she walked. Eyes of deep black peered out at the world. Her lips were cracked, dried from the sun. She had no clothes, only her long flowing earth-colored hair. She was not human.

Some called her Powa'ha or Water-air Spirit. These spirits will save a person who throws themselves off of a mesa into a river or lake. The Powa'ha reach out to this falling person to gently place them on the ground, unhurt. My people know her as A'she-u'u or Salt Arroyo Spirit.

Two men and a woman were walking down the gorge to Yunque-yunque. Cautiously, they approached this strange figure. Startled the men turned from her as she appeared as a woman with no clothing. The woman put a blanket around this being's frail body. The woman told the men to go ahead, she would catch up with them. Sitting together, the woman tried to understand why this stranger was alone and naked. A'she-u'u or Salt Woman did not know how to communicate. Frustrated, the woman left her there, alone.

As the woman met up with her male companions, she licked her lips. There was a strange taste. A good taste. It was the taste of salt. Noticing that her hands had the powdered skin from the stranger, she smelled them. She smelled salt. The men asked what she was doing and they in turn tasted her hands. They liked the flavor of the powder. When they hurried back to find the stranger, she was gone.

Salt Woman walked along the Rio Grande. She heard people, but she avoided them. They spoke a language she did not understand. Soon, she was hungry. Yunque-yunque was having a feast day with dancing and food. Wrapped in the blanket, she entered the north side of the Pueblo. People stared at her. A grandmother came to her, "Let me get you something to wear for soon it will be hot and you will be hot in the blanket. Come, come with me."

Salt Woman had no knowledge of what the grandmother said, but she followed. Grandmother urged A'she-u'u into the building. Salt Woman would not enter. The old woman came out and took her hand. Talking kindly to Salt Woman, she led her into the front room. There was no one else in the room. Grandmother took the blanket off of A'she-u'u. Using a ladle, she poured fresh water onto a woven cloth to wash the filth off of this strange young woman. The cloth soon turned white. Grandmother pulled a simple Pueblo dress over Salt Woman's head, over her shoulders, and pulled it down to her ankles. There on the floor around A'she-u'u was a pile of wet powder. Grandmother ignored it for Salt Woman smiled with gratitude. The old woman handed her the blanket, telling her she would need it in the winter.

Pulling Salt Woman into the large room, Grandmother prepared a bowl of food for her. There was meat with different kinds of baked squash called mowa or salt bush meal. This was mixed with hot ash for there was hardly any other food grown after the heavy rains. Cool water from the streams was to drink. Salt Woman sat as she was shown and quickly ate all the food put in front of her. Other families arrived bringing different foods. They watched as this strange woman gulped bowl after bowl of posole, boiled beans, and dried jerky and fresh bread pieces.

Suddenly, the stranger stopped eating. She stood at the table to put her thumb and index finger to her nose. Taking a deep breath, the strange woman blew mucous from her nose into her palm. Then she flung the wet matter over the food on the table. As the mucous flew across the table, it turned into a fine white powder.

People jumped back from the table. Loud yelling and screaming brought the Elders into the room. The guardians of the Pueblo, the Mudheads entered to carry this woman, hugging her blanket, out of the village. They put her down far from the people, near a dry arroyo.

At Yunque-yunque some of the Elders tasted the food with her dried mucous on it. No one else would eat. The Elders took the dried mucous from the table, sweeping it into a sap covered basket. This white powder was felt to be a spiritual gift brought to the people by a Sacred Spirit. The older women, being brave began to use the white powder on thinly sliced meat. As the meat dried in the sun, coated with the powder, they found it did not spoil. White powder was stirred into the squash stews. Meals tasted richer and the stews lasted longer. Now, the people wanted Salt Woman. They searched for her, but she had moved to another place.

Runners were sent to find this strange woman. News arrived of a woman made of white powder visiting Ku'onwi'keji, a village near Santa Clara Pueblo. Ku'onwi'keji isn't there anymore for the people were killed and later were initiated into other Pueblos. Again, there was the story of a strange woman entering the village to spread her mucous over the food. Women met at places of trade to talk about the strange woman, known as Salt Woman or A'she-u'u.

Salt Woman appeared to float quickly ahead of those who were trying to find her. The place known as Te'eonwi'keji near Oso Creek, had a family who told Pueblo runners that she was seen walking south across the canyon probably on her way to K'apo'unwi or Santa Clara Pueblo. A man with gray feathers told someone they had seen a strange woman in Pueblo dress climbing into Toba'qwak'aento'iwe or the place where there is a cave near San Ildefonso Pueblo. Men were sent to find her, but again she was not there.

Two young boys, hunting for quail, told the Elders of seeing a strange woman walking along Paeqwaen'kwage or Deer Tail Mesa. They described this figure to be thin and bent as she walked into the winds that blew hard at that altitude. Again, men went out to find her. Again, she was not there.

On trading day near Tsampije'I'pin'f or Jemez Pueblo Mountain, there was news of her coming to their feast day. They explained how after she had eaten, she had sprayed her mucous across the food on the table. This time she was carried away on horseback to Si'po'pe or the Place of Stone Lions near Shi'wi or Zuni Pueblo. The riders said they dumped her in a sandy arroyo to the north of the R'pae'po'kote or Rabbit Mountain, which is closer to Cochiti not Zuni. My grandfather calls this place Mesa Prieta. The riders said she could live in a cave halfway up Mesa Prieta, if she could find it. This cave is called Tobaqwata'ndwi'i'isi or Painted Cave where ancestors once lived and colored the walls with their stories.

No one could find A'she-u'u. Many believed Salt Woman traveled on the north wind that blew to the south. News came of her from the village of Okupinf or Turtle Mountain that she was not welcome. A trader from Kepita or Picuris told of her being at Kiutawe or Jemez just days ago. Then a man rode into Oke O'wenge to visit friends saying this Salt Woman was definitely at Tsi'pi'ja, a village close to Shi'wi or Zuni.

An'paekwijo or Old Salt Woman was seen by a man in the field of Kueesche or Laguna Pueblo. She was walking quickly toward A-qo or Acoma Pueblo. No one from Acoma remembers hearing anything about her. Zuni people talk of her visiting their feast day. She spread her nose mucous all over the feast table in one home, but the family had heard of her and her salt. They tried to keep her in Zuni, but she wouldn't stay.

Old Ones say she moved without her feet actually touching the ground. The water of the Old Lake south of Zuni accepted her into its waters. Her spirit is still there. Her salt still floats on the surface. She will not give salt to women only to men who show respect to her and the water spirits. My older brother went to her for salt during a testing. He came back with a block of salt. He wouldn't talk about what happened there. This is all I know about her.

6 Old Story of Salt Woman (Cochiti)

There have been eight Cochiti Pueblos or villages that my people moved from and built. Old Salt Woman had a grandson. These two had nothing. Nothing at all except the simple clothes they wore. Salt Woman was thin. Her spine was bent as if she was folding over to go back into the earth. Her grandson was also thin. His eyes were deep brown and to look into his eyes, one only perceived a vacant stare. Both of them had crusty skin. Their skin was dark from the sun, dried from the wind and cracked. The grandson had bleeding sores on the back of his neck.

Salt Woman smelled acrid as if she had washed in strong acid. Her brown hair was matted at the back of her head. Her attitude was one of urgency. When she came into the Pueblo, she hurried dragging her grandson beside her. She held him tightly by the wrist. He stumbled at her side as if he wanted to run, but didn't know how. When they came to Cochiti and quickly moved from house to house, the owners of the homes turned them away.

The women were busy cooking and the men didn't know them nor was this strange pair trusted. At that time the people didn't know about salt.

Salt Woman appeared to be an old woman. She was dressed in torn leather rags from deer skins. They were dirty and dark. Her hair long and wild, uncombed and unwashed, made people reject her entrance into their homes. Her feet were calloused and bare. The skin on her legs was scarred from walking miles through all kinds of bushes and weeds. Her hands were filthy from dirt and digging for roots to eat. She had dark eyes, sunken into her leathery sunburned face. Her lips were cracked and stained from berry juice. Her long arms were also scarred and burned dark from many months, years in the sun.

The small boy constantly whined and his nose ran down to his chin, even though he wiped it with his arm constantly. There were tear tracks down his cheeks for he was always crying and sniffling. He was a sad little boy. Many times when he fell behind, Salt Woman would grab his wrist to drag him along behind her. The Pueblo people found them to be hideous. As the leaves fell in the fall and as branches broke and scratched at the earth, Salt Woman and her grandson dug for water, ripped dried berries from withered branches and hunkered into hand dug arroyo shelters to survive.

There was no rest for these two. They were constantly hungry, extremely filthy and had nowhere to call a home or a place to rest peacefully. Going to each Pueblo Feast Day, one after the other seeking food, hoping for shelter, but rarely finding any for Salt Woman had this particular trait. Before she would enter a home to eat, she would lift her dress and show the people the inside of her thigh. Taking a knife from her belt, she would scrape the white skin from her thigh and offer it to the people as a trade for the food. Knowledge of her nasty habit spread quickly. Soon no Pueblo would allow her to enter for the feast.

Salt Woman's thin, crusty body was of salt. When Salt Woman and her grandson had gone to all the houses within a Pueblo, begging for food only to be sent away hungry, she became angry. The children had no fear of her or the boy. Out from under her dress Salt Woman in her anger would pull out a large crystal. It was white and glistened in the sunlight. Sitting near the children, she would sing to the crystal. In the sunlight the flashing crystal would begin to hum with her song.

When all the children came to see the magic crystal that Salt Woman had in her hand, she would lead them to a tall pinion tree. There she told each of the children to take hold of a branch of the tree and climb. The higher they climbed, the more willing she would be to let them hold her crystal. The children climbed higher and higher, at some of the villages the pinion tree would bend with the weight of the children. Slowly, turning, smiling at the eager climbers, she would lift the crystal above her head to chant. The magic crystal would sing out a high pitched song. Her chanting would become faster and faster as she watched the children. When she stopped, the children were Chaparral Pinion Jays. Chirping frantically, the birds would fly back to the village.

Parents and family would yell and throw rocks at the frantic birds attacking them. In late afternoon, when the families came searching for their children, all they would find would be a pine tree filled with crying Chaparral Jays. The people would run after Salt Woman, calling to her, begging her to tell them where their children were.

Salt Woman would shake her head, "When we were in your pueblo, no one would invite us to stay and eat. Your children are now Chaparral Jays. You shall eat alone."

Salt Woman and her grandson went south, stopping at Santa Domingo Pueblo, where they were fed well. After they had eaten and were leaving, Salt Woman said, "I am thankful for being given food to eat," She left them some of her flesh. The people of the house ate it with their bread and meat. It tasted good, salty.

"At Cochiti," Salt Woman told them, "They treated me badly and when I left, I took all the children outside the pueblo and changed them into Chaparral Jays roosting them in pinion trees. But to you I am grateful. I will go southeast and stay there and if any of you want more of my flesh you will find it at that place, and when you come to gather salt, let there be no laughing, no singing, nothing of that kind. Be quiet and clean." She left Santo Domingo and went to Mount Taylor.

There she prayed and left her grandson to watch over the eagles and ravens in the sky. Alone, she walked to Salt Lake by Zuni. Walking into the lake, she left the trials of life on land. Men now go to the lake to retrieve salt. We pray that she has found peace in the water and no longer suffers. Zuni Salt Lake is where we get salt today.

7   Story of Salt Woman (Isleta)

Salt Woman is called out with song at the end of October. The Auki'i (or Chief Assistant) sits at the right-hand of the Chief. The Toaptadelopi'i is his assistant who sits at the left-hand of the Chief. Guarding the door of the kiva are the War Captains. The Chief is from the four different Corn Clans; the yellow corn, black corn, blue corn, and mixed color corn groups. It used to be that the ceremony was every year, but when the church came we had to do this ceremony every three to five years and we did it quietly. The Corn Chief would ask the Hunt Chief who would ask the Town Chief for permission to hold the call for Salt Woman. The Hunt Chief would then go into retreat for four days, to perform ceremony at noon on the fourth day. Blowing smoke into his medicine bowl, he then would blow smoke toward the mountains to blind the deer. Finally, he whistled to bring the deer. Hunters would hide near the Pueblo ready to hunt. The live deer being enchanted by the Hunt Chief would walk straight to the Pueblo. Hunters killed them successfully to bring lasting food for the winter.

One February, it was very cold with no rain or snow, just constant wind, drying the land. The Hunt Chief or Humahude called the War Chiefs to come to his house. He told them to draw a circle in the middle of the floor in the front room with yellow pollen. Humahude took a handful of goose feathers to crush them into the center of the circle of yellow pollen. This, we knew was a map for the deer. He sang softly, then he began to call out with the voice of a bear and a mountain lion at the same time. While singing, he would motion with his arm, telling the War Chief to open the door of the room to the outside, facing east.

Into the house, came a huge buck deer with a head of large antlers. Humahude kept on singing while signing for the War Chief to close the door. The buck walked into the circle of pollen and once in the center, Humahude closed the gap of the circle with pollen. The buck snorted, but stood still. Humahude took his K'oata, or man-shaped stone and gently tapped the buck on the forehead. The buck dropped, dead. Humahude told the War Chiefs to butcher it, cutting pieces for the medicine men with a piece to be given to the Cacique or Town Chief. The people had food and did not starve that frozen spring.

The people needed salt for their food and for their strength. The ceremony to bring Salt Woman out of the mountains and into the village was one of a process. Again this was done during the end of October, as I said before. This ceremony of a single day and a night was done by the Town Chief, who is also called the Cacique. It was performed in the Black Eyes Roundhouse or the kiva above ground. People from the village were invited into the Salt Woman Ceremony since it started in the daytime. If there were people in the kiva who had bad thoughts or who had done something not within their tradition, the Humahude and his assistants would turn them into animals.

It is said the Humahude was given this power by Salt Woman for she sees and knows all. If a person killed a snake and told no one or hadn't asked for forgiveness, he would be turned into a snake. Persons who were mean and would not help others, would be turned into porcupines or snakes. There were some people who told lies to hurt and harm others purposely, they were turned into poisonous frogs or toads. Still there were others who had done practices without permission or had hurt others. These people were turned into animals, snakes, toads, or bird-like-vultures to fly away. Salt Woman had great powers even from a distance.

When people were hungry and had nothing to offer others during Salt Woman Ceremony, they would ask a person to give them their moccasins. The moccasins would be turned into meat and passed around for the people to eat. All of this was great magic. The knowledge of her powers were known to all. Even if she could not be seen, this did not mean that she wasn't there to use her magic.

There was a time when some children made fun of Salt Woman. Hiding from her, they watched her scrape some of her skin into a basket. While she handed the basket to the people, who were thankful for the salt, the children laughed at her and called her names. After this, Salt Woman stayed away from the village and would only come if she was called. Respect and Honor were needed for her to appear. The children soon learned that the people suffered without her salt.

Many bad, hurtful people would not come to the Salt Woman ceremony for they were fearful of her judgment. They could be turned into an animal or reptile. It was important for Salt Woman to hear as many voices as possible, calling her back to the village. It was the loud sound of respect that brought her. If there weren't many people singing, she would not hear the song. Once she heard the loud voices, she knew of the people's need and she would return to them.

The meat and much of the food needed salt in order to stay healthy through the cold winters. The strength of the people's voices would bring her into the Black Eyes Roundhouse, or kiva. A bright vision of a woman in white, all white, like a large piece of ice would appear in the middle of the Black Eyes kiva. Gliding down the ladder, hearing the song, she would enter into the large room with a fire in the middle. No feathers were used, just the voices of respectful people. There, she would place a large basket filled with powdered salt beside the fire.

On the opposite side of the fire would be another basket filled with glass beads and turquoise. Glass beads worn around her neck, stopped evil from getting close to her. Turquoise cleansed her body, preventing evil from entering into her, which would spoil the salt. The people gave her this basket out of appreciation. Thankful for the gifts in the basket, Salt Woman would hold it close to her as she glided up the ladder, leaving the people to sing their praises of her and their gratitude for her gifts. When the mercantiles came to the villages and Pueblos, the traders brought in round containers of Morton's salt. Salt Woman stopped coming when her songs were sung. Perhaps she brings her salt to a different village for she only gives salt to those who are in need. Salt Woman is kind, but a woman who demands respect.

8 Salt Woman Traditional (Acoma)

When the people were living at Kacikatcut'ya or the White House Place in the north, there was a woman named Mina Koya. Mina Koya was known to be a bitter angry woman. No one was sure where she had come from or where she was supposed to go. Mina Koya was short and wore a manta that was torn, frayed, and covered with dirt. Her caramel colored eyes matched her thinning wiry hair. Long fingernails protruded from her thick fingers, giving her a fearful appearance. She cackled and grunted whenever asked a question. The people didn't want her around their children or in their homes. She had no man to provide her with food. No one knew where she had come from, all they knew was she appeared and at times wouldn't leave until she was brought what she wanted. People believed her to be magical. This made them afraid of her. Going from home to home in each village, she would beg, pointing her long fingernails at the children. Mothers would quickly bring her whatever she wanted just for her to go away and leave them alone.

Many village people argued with her, trying to get her to leave, usually this didn't work. If no one brought her food or were goaded by her, she would start chanting. Frightened of her voice and her curses, they would wrap food for her, asking her to leave. Onward she would go to the next village. When the villages realized how her threats worked, they would close their doors or completely ignore her and she would eventually leave. No matter how hungry she was, few people would give her food. Once she received food, she would stay at the door and chant until more food was given. Families learned to not give her food at all.

The temperament of Mina Koya was to argue with each person she met. Grandfather said she would scold and curse people while walking on the road. My grandmother said, she was bitter because she was made of salt. Some said their grandparents were frightened of her. If she was invited into the home, she would spit on their food. Once she came into a family's cooking room and she spit into the stew on the fire. Since she was dirty and had a nasty temper, no one trusted her or wanted to have anything to do with her.

Mina Koya sometimes would find a widow who was lonely and in need of company. They would allow her to stay, but soon her true personality would arrive and she would be thrown out of the home by clan members or friends of the widow. Pueblo life is made up as one community. There is not one person who would be more or less important than the whole. Mina Koya did not help anyone. Her total concern was for herself and for herself alone. This is not the way of the Pueblo life.

There came a time when she disappeared from the Northern Pueblos. Moving from village to village, begging and cursing kept her hungry. Some would let her stay in their field huts if the weather was bad or it was cold, but they preferred for her to keep going. Pushed out of village after village, Mina Koya kept moving south. Some say she walked into Mexico and she is still there today, living in a forest with food and fish. Others say she traveled and as she traveled, her body slowly disappeared along with her anger until there was nothing left but a warm breeze. An old man in our village said she stopped at Shi-wi or what is known today as Zuni. There, outside of the village is a large lake. Mina Koya stopped to look at her reflection in the water of the lake. Disgusted by how dirty she was, she decided to wash. Going into the lake, she turned the lake into salt. Today, this lake is known as Zuni Salt Lake, but that could be another story!

9   La Loba or Wolf Woman (Zia)

La Loba was Wolf Woman who wandered on the flatlands and the barrancas of New Mexico, searching for wolf bones. Many times warriors would try to catch her by using traps, but she would either jump through the trap or she would disappear. Wolf Woman was not a tall woman nor was she large. She was short, fast, and very thin like a wolf. Her hair was long and was the color of white mixed with gray. Her feet were bare and her eyes were dark, shining wild in the moonlight.

My grandfather and I came across her on the flats. We were hunting for deer. It was in the fall. The cold winds had just started. The deer were moving down from the high forested areas into the flatland, nearer to the water for one last graze on sweet grass and to drink cool river water before heading southwest to warmer plains. My grandfather was squatting, hiding low. There were chamisa bushes around him. The yellow chamisa is poisonous to insects and some animals. Don't know why people plant it in their yard, makes them sick. Anyway, my grandfather was low, close to the ground. There was no wind, just a very slight breeze that barely moved the rabbit bush.

I was opposite him, down low, too. I was lying flat on the ground on a small sandy hill with a cluster of rabbit bush as my guardian. All I could see of grandfather was the tip of his arrow. We could hear the deer moving slowly forward. They were cautious, which made us cautious. Their hooves were making some noise on the stones in the arroyo to my right. Grandfather lifted his hand over the chamisa. That was our signal to freeze, not move, not shoot our arrows, but to stay absolutely still. Something was threatening the deer and could possibly be a threat to us. Pointing my arrow tip into the sandy mound in front of me, I closed my eyes to say a small prayer to the Great Spirit.

The breeze stopped. There were maybe four large clouds overhead. The sky was a soft chalk blue, almost white. I dug my feet into the sand, hoping that whatever was coming would not see me, that I was invisible. Almost as soon as I thought this, I heard my grandfather whistle softly. There to my left, blending in with the white and green of the rabbit bush was a figure. Slowly, my eyes adjusted and there, almost as a dream, was a small woman. She was sniffing at the ground, moving closer and closer to me. Hunched over with her knees bent, back bowed, nose to the ground, she stopped. Suddenly, her hands started frantically digging up the sand, shooting it behind her from between her legs. Her hair wild and matted, flew around her head.

I dared not even blink. I was breathing through my nose quietly. The deer did not approach her. Then as fast as she had dug, she stopped. Her eyes darted around her. Her nose was sniffing eagerly. I did not even inhale, but watched. Slowly, she lifted out of the sand several bleached bones. Amazingly, she licked each one as she placed it in a form. Once the bones were as she wanted them to be, she pushed back her hair to howl. It was a blood curdling howl. The deer raced away. Birds stopped singing.

When she finished there was a deafening silence. Reaching up to the sky, she opened her mouth to sing. Her voice was soft, soft as the breeze that touched her. Her voice slowly and carefully became louder and louder. The breeze turned into a gentle wind. The gentle wind slowly swirled around her. Her voice was hypnotic, as if she was calling the dead.

Then, silence. Crouched with her hands and feet on the ground, she continued to lick the bones in front of her. Moving from one bone to the other, she would stop and sing her eerie song. There was no melody, just sounds, her hands lifting bones from the hole in the ground in front of her. Again, the bones were laid out in the proper order. I can't remember if her hands were furry or if they were like ours, for she moved quickly. The song, the bones being put out in order, the song, her hair flowing around her head, and at times the sand flying out behind her. This was all quite surprising and happened quickly. There were ribs, hip bones, finally a skull of a dog. Her nose now was covered with sand as she licked the white bones clean and sang.

Magically, the ground around us shook. Out of nowhere came a dust storm, but it swirled only around her and the bones. Quickly it surrounded her, twirling round and round and round and round, dirt flying, flinging against me and everything within twenty feet of her. Suddenly it stopped. The air was dead quiet. Not a movement.

Blinking now with amazement, there in front of this strange woman was a wolf. A white wolf stood in front of her, licking her nose. She nudged it with her nose and then the two of them sped off out of sight. I jumped, as my grandfather burst out laughing.

He slapped his thigh and ran over to me. "Did you see that? My grandson, did you see what just happened? We were blessed, she trusted us! She knew we were here, she must have known we were here! She trusted us to see her magic! Did you see what she did?" Grandfather was now doing a jig in the middle of the flats between the rabbit bush and the chamisa.

I was stunned. "Grandfather, what did she do? How did she do that magic?" "Grandson, we have been blessed by her. She trusted us to see her and her magic!" He grabbed me by my elbow to swing me around him. "Grandson, the spirits have given us a sign! We are now blessed."

Finally, I got away from him. "Grandfather, what she did was amazing! She took some wolf bones that were buried in sand and brought them to life as a wolf. Grandfather, is she the Wolf Woman?"

I walked over to the hole in the sand. Her footprints could still be seen. The paw prints of the wolf that loped away were visible as well. Kneeling down in the sand, I lifted some of it to my face to smell. The sand smelled like rotten meat. Grandfather hurried to me.

He hit my hand and the sand flew away. "No, don't touch anything of hers. This is magic. We are not to mess with the spirit world nor are we to question it. Hurry, let's go home and tell your grandmother. She will be delighted. When she was twelve years old, she saw the Wolf Woman and she was blessed. Come, let's go!"

The deer were forgotten that day, but not the next. When we went out hunting the following day, we had six other young men with us. Grandfather was grinning from ear to ear at our blessing. Our hunt that day was good, even though I was cautiously worried about her coming across our path. I have hunted for many years after that, many times not far from that same place and never again did I see the Wolf Woman.

There were some young girls who went out to gather yucca roots who came across her, but she was gone before they could see her change bones into a wolf. There is a Wolf Woman who was seen over by Acoma. She helps people who are lost or small children who run away. She guards them and shows them the way to safety. Somehow I do believe that it is the White Wolf Woman we saw that day. Some ask me if I thought she was beautiful. I can't say she was beautiful, she looked ragged, tired, and frantic when I saw her. She was bringing one of her kind back to life. It is a serious job to bring something back to life and it is something that had to be done quickly. She must hunt and eat what the wolves eat for she is certainly one of their kind.

Now, at the trading post I did hear of stories where the Spaniards saw her and tried to catch her. There is a story of a Spaniard who wanted to marry her for he was in love with her spirit. They tried all kinds of ways to catch her, but none of them worked. There is the story of one man shooting at her and she bled, but he never found her. Perhaps she has a way of healing quickly. This is the only story that I know of Zia Pueblo, the smallest pueblo here in New Mexico. Traditionally we are blessed with Strong Spirits.

10   The Old Woman of the Spring
(Cheyenne)

My family is from the Cheyenne people, this is our story about water and the magic that water can bring to those who believe. The Cheyenne know the universe is in different layers. The people see the universe from the Earth. Above the Earth is Heammahestonev. Life below the earth is known as Aktunov. Along the surface of the earth is a thin layer of air. This is called Taxtavo and it is a special spirit gift to the humans. This air allows breathing and allows life. Above the air layer is Setovo or Nearer to the Sky Space. This is the earth's atmosphere and is known to modern science. In Setovo there are clouds, wind, birds and the holy places where we can go to pray up on the mountains.

Above what we know here on earth is the Blue Sky Space or Aktovo. Sun, moon, stars and the Milky Way live there. The earth has two layers. The first is the very thin place. This supports life as we know it. It is only as deep as the roots of trees or the deepness of the flowing rivers and lakes holding water. This is known as Votoso. Beneath Votoso is Aktunov or the Deep Earth.

Each level is filled with spiritual forces, being the home of a spirit that has magical parts, which visit us on our concept of earth. Blue Sky Space is the home of the Sun. Cheyenne call it esehe or Day Sun. Every morning, Sun is born and anyone can see it. The Sun is the Sun Spirit of the Boss called Atovsz. Sun is both a thing and a spirit. Atovsz is powerful and can take on man's form. Moon is known as Taesehe or Night Sun. Night Sun is born in the west every twenty-eight nights. Everyone can see Night Sun. Visible moon has a spirit called Ameonito or Moon Spirit of Night Boss. This can make an appearance of a human as well if it wishes to favor someone.

Certain planets can be human as well. Morning Star and Evening Star are strong spirits. Morning Star and Evening Stars are close in power to Sun Spirit and Moon Spirit. Some stars have very important purposes. The Milky Way is seen on clear night skies over the plains. This is called ekutsihimmiyo or the Hanging Road and is suspended between the Blue Sky Space and Earth Spirit. It is the road the dead travel to live in the other world.

There are many spirits who live in different levels of life between the lower earth and the sky. These are Heammahestov for they are all knowing. High Good Heammawihio is the Wise One Above. Wihio means spider. Spider spins webs and Spider goes up and down an invisible path as if it is walking on nothing. Wihio appears and allows a person to have the ability to use their mind to go higher or lower in consciousness. This takes great training and much learning for this is to have Spiritual wisdom. Heammawihio is the Top Boss. He knows more about how to do things than any other Spirit or human. Heammawihio left earth and moved to live in the sky. Sun is also Heammawihio, but more so for he can burn the earth and radiates heat. When the ceremonial pipe is lit, the smoking is for him.

Beneath the surface of the Earth is Aktuno or Deep Earth and this place has its own spirituality. The Dark Deep Earth is female and is governed by Heammawihio's Deep Earth brother known as Aktunowihio. Women get their strength for healing and birthing in the night with the help of Aktunowihio.

The Cheyenne believe the universe follows a long horizontal plane of order. This is divided into four cardinal directions; south, east, north and west. The south and the east are red with warmth and light and usually green with growing plants. The north is cold with the white of winter. West is blue-black for it holds death and the healing of night. Each is the holder of certain spirits and each color symbolizes the major direction and seasonal changes.

When the Cheyenne were still in the north, they camped in a large circle. At one end of this circle, there was an opening that led to a spring that flowed from a hillside. The water needed for the camp came from that spring. The women would say a blessing each time they took water from that spring in the hillside. The people were there to ask the Spirits to send them buffalo for there were none to be found and the parents, the children, and the elders were all starving. The women were thankful for the water from this spring.

One day, when the men were dancing, asking the Spirits for buffalo, two young men approached. They told the dancers to stop their dancing. These two young men said they had come to play hoops with the Cheyenne and if they were clever enough to shoot their javelin through a hoop this would make the spirits happy and at least make the people feel more celebratory. The youth gathered up their red and black hoops and four long sticks, two red and two black, and these they threw at the hoop as it rolled along within the circle. The team whose sticks went through the most hoops, while the hoop was moving, won. The people were whooping and calling, feeling better than they had in a long time. These two men were pleased to see the people enjoying themselves.

As night approached, these two men pulled on their buffalo hides to return to their own camp. It was at this time, they noticed each of them were wearing their buffalo hides with the fur on the outside. This was most unusual for the weather was warm, yet they were not hot in their hide coats. The two young men curiously thought of how they had obtained these buffalo hide coats as they walked through the water above the spring. People gathered around them to hear how they had obtained their great buffalo coats.

The men explained how they would walk through the stream again to find out where the buffalo coats had come from and to return with the information. The young man from the north went into the spring first. Then the young man from the south walked into the water. Near the entrance, sat an old woman who carried much wisdom with her. Silently with long wooden spoons, she stirred food cooking in two separate earthen pots. The smell of the delicious food made the young men stop and watch her.

Smiling at them, she said, "In one pot there is buffalo meat and in the other pot, I am cooking corn."

They watched her. As she stirred the pots became larger and the food grew in abundance. The grandmother's braided black hair glistened in the firelight. When she smiled, her face wrinkled. Her long print dress was stained from cutting meat, cooking and being too close to the firepots. Pointing to a blanket beside her, she said, "Grandsons, come here, sit by me."

When they sat down, she ladled two large spoonfuls of food into two rounded wooden bowls. The steaming bowls of food was handed to them. Smiling, she said, "You two are very thin, you must be hungry. Eat for this will help make you fat!"

Each of the young men willingly ate, until one of them stopped to say, "There are people near here who are starving. They have not had any food all summer. The animals are missing and the fields they seeded have no plants because of the drought."

The other young man nodded in agreement, "The people on the other side of the stream have nothing more to trade for food. Many of the children have lost their parents to hunger. Would it be possible to share this food with the people who have nothing to eat?"

The old woman shook her head, "It is sad when the people forget to show respect for what they need. The loss of the Elders left the younger people lost. When hunters show respect to the animals they kill in the hunt, more animals will arrive. If there is no respect shown, animals will disappear."

Pointing with a long wooden spoon, she told the young men, "Ask these people who are hungry to look to the south at sunset. Large animals will appear. If they hunt to kill animals, they need to say a prayer of respect before they take the meat. Some will see ponies, deer, antelope and bear." Shaking her head, she said, "First, these people must eat to have strength."

Turning, she pointed to the north to say, "These people will see low swampland and this is where they can grow corn. It is important for them to keep some of the kernels of the corn and plant them only in the spring for corn will not grow in the fall. The people must not eat all of the corn kernels for this will not allow them to have anything to plant in the spring. Also, it is important to thank the earth for the corn, otherwise, they will have none."

The wise woman told them, "All that I have told you shall be yours in the future. Tonight, I will allow the buffalo to be restored to you for you are respectful and you listen. You must take this pot of meat and give it to the people to eat. First to eat, will be all the men from the youngest to the oldest. Any orphan boys must not eat. Then all the women and children are to eat, but not the orphan girls. When everyone has finished eating, the orphan boys and the orphan girls may eat."

She handed them a pot of buffalo meat. "Again, here is a pot of corn. This must be eaten in the same order as the buffalo meat. Do not let the orphans eat with the others of the buffalo and the corn or there will not be no food at all. Do you understand?" The two young men nodded for they did understand.

They knew this was very great magic. The wise woman led them to the place where they could leave the flowing spring water. When they walked out onto the land, they were painted red with yellow bird feathers tied in their hair on their heads. They went to the people, who ate as they were told of the meat and corn. There was more than enough food for all the people even the orphans. This was good.

At sunset, the hunters went onto a rise and searched the horizon for the buffalo. Soon they noticed one buffalo jump out of the spring water to gallop off onto the plateau. It rolled and played on the dry land. After it came another and another. The buffalo came out quickly and continued to arrive all night long until the whole of the plateau and the plains were covered with them, running, rolling, galloping, and playing.

Soon, they saw antelope, deer, and wild ponies grazing on the grass-lands. The Cheyenne hunters went out and hunted on foot for they ran fast. Each hunter knelt at the head of the killed animal to say a prayer. This is how it must be or there will be hunger. The people had an abundance of meat. The hunters did not kill more than what was needed.

In the spring, the people moved their camp to the north, to a low swampland. There they planted the corn kernels. By fall they had strong corn stalks bearing two or four ears of corn. The people planted corn every year after this. One spring after the corn planting, the Cheyenne went out on a buffalo hunt. When they returned, they found the corn fields had been stripped. A raiding tribe had stolen all their corn. There were no kernels to be found on the ground or anywhere. After this, the Cheyenne had no corn for a long time. It is good to listen to wise grandmothers.

11 Woman Who Killed Huge Bat
(Guiana)

A long, long while ago, an immense bat spread terror among the people of Makusis. Huge Bat lived on a mountain top high, high up on a mountaintop. His feathers along his wings were purple black and his teeth were sharp as silver plated spears. A long tongue was covered with a thick orange slime. Huge brown eyes circled in orange red peered out at the world, darting from one place to another in search of food. Huge Bat had a Huge Family that lived high on the mountaintop in a cave. Many a hunter had tried to scale the mountain to kill Huge Bat, but few survived Bat's teeth.

Huge Bat usually came out at nightfall to catch and eat the people who lived in the valley below. All the Makusis lived in fear of this Huge Bat. People cried and worried, scared to leave their homes for fear they might be eaten. Even if they stayed near their homes, Huge Bat could swoop down to devour them. Children were rarely allowed outside and the men were unable to fish or hunt for fear of being eaten.

Medicine men who were strong and wise worked all the magic they knew to try and stop this Huge Bat, but Bat kept coming to feed on them. There were times when Bat came two or three times a night to hunt for people, taking them up onto his mountaintop cave.

An old wise woman who was brave decided she had to do something. No, she decided she must do a task to stop Bat from destroying all of her people, her family, and her village. At high noon one day, she walked to the edge of the mountain. There she sat and studied the mountaintop where the Huge Bat lived. She thought about this Bat and his greedy hunger. Praying to the Spirits, she asked for a plan. The wise woman knew she was not strong nor was she young. Her daughters and granddaughters had told her of her weaknesses and her faults, but this wise woman knew that inside of herself there was courage. She had the strength to save her children and her grandchildren. Nothing could take this determination from her.

On that special night, this old wise woman sat in the middle of the village holding a covered fire stick. Her daughters and granddaughters called to her, telling her she was crazy and would die. This wise woman only smiled and waited. The frightened village people hid in their houses, peering out at her, watching her, for they saw she was brave in her duty.

As the clouds covered the moon, the people heard the Huge Bat winging fast and furiously toward the village. He swooped over the old wise woman as she sat in the middle of village before a fire. The old wise woman kept her fire stick covered. Huge Bat dug his sharp talons deep into her spine to grasp her. The first pain of the talons was extreme. As the talons dug more deeply into her body, she struggled not to cry out for help. Huge Bat carried her off into the dark of the night to his nest high on the mountaintop.

The wise old woman waited for Huge Bat to open his mouth and place her onto his tongue. As his talons shoved her body between his teeth, she pulled the cover off the fire stick, letting the flames from the fire stick explode on Huge Bat's tongue. Thick sticky saliva burst into hot liquid fire, spewing flames onto the nest, burning everything around them.

In the morning, the people cautiously climbed the mountain carrying spears, knives and flint. At mid-day, they found the bones of the Huge Bat and the Bat family. The old wise woman had courage, she may have been killed, but she will always be remembered.

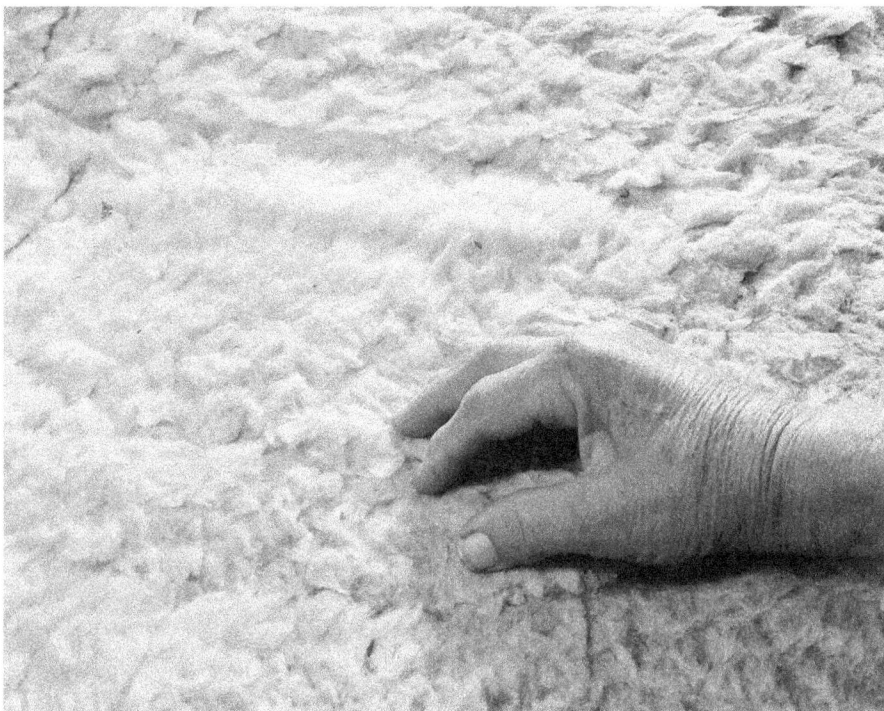

12   The Sheepskin (Hopi)

Being old helps you to remember. There was a time when no stores were near. A time when we were all too poor to have anything to trade. We had sheep. Lots of sheep. This meant that we would not go hungry nor would we ever be cold. We had mutton for food and had woven blankets of sheep's wool for warmth. There were those who died and left us with only memories both good and bad.

My daughter, you are young yet. You have your whole life ahead of you even though you are married and have four children. Here on the reservation, there are not many who are old for many died before they were able to reach old age. They were killed by disease, alcohol or were left behind and ignored. Sadness and loneliness are sometimes the worst killers of my generation. You are here and for this I am most grateful. You bring me hope and love with every visit. Each smile and each hug prolongs my life for love is the best medicine that exists. One cannot live without love and kindness and generosity.

Now, this is for you to understand. Here is your grandfather's sheepskin. He gave this to your grandmother. She died too young. She was dearly loved.

Feel it, feel how soft is, here.

This was your grandmother's.

She would sit here by the fire.

She would hold it in her lap like this.

She would stroke it up and down.

She would hold it close to her bosom and laugh.

Feel how worn the back is.

This sheepskin was her first.

Her husband took it from their first lamb slaughtered.

He cured the skin, gave her the meat to fix for dinner and I am sure he watched as she smiled.

Her smile, her smile made you feel loved.

Her smile showed her crooked teeth, cracked from breaking pinion nuts.

Her smile wrinkled the worn brown skin of her cheeks.

Her smile lit her brown eyes to a radiant glow.

Her smile gave you love.

The sheepskin is still here, after all this time.

Your uncles were washed, diapered, nursed on this sheepskin.

Your father put his head on this sheepskin when he napped.

I cried on this sheepskin when your grandmother died.

This is your sheepskin now, this is for you.

Feel it, feel how soft it is, feel how soft this is, feel its warmth.

This is for you, come let me see you smile.

13 Grandfather's Story and Salt Woman (Zuni)

Walking into the kitchen, the first person seen was the frail elderly man sitting in a wheelchair. The wheelchair appeared large, huge. The elderly man was small, sitting on a fat pillow. He was bent, crippled with arthritis. Lifting his chin, but not able to lift his head, he smiled. Dark brown eyes with gray circles around his pupils were deep set. Wrinkles around his mouth and chin grew deeper as he smiled. Thin gray hair braided tightly fell from each side of his balding head. Gnarled fingers slightly shook in his lap. The red and gray plaid shirt had been freshly ironed and starched. White sleeves buttoned at his wrists hung loose. Dark blue pants had also been ironed to have a razor pleat at the front to crease neatly over his bent knees. Moccasins worn, frayed at the top, were tied at his ankles.

Bernadette put out her hand, "This is our Sendo, our Grandfather. He tells us he has a story to tell. We are too busy to listen because we have work, school and television to keep us busy, hah! He just doesn't want us to listen."

"No one listens to an old man." Grandfather's soft voice echoed in the small kitchen. The rich smell of posole filled the air as it bubbled on the wood cooking stove behind him. A large container of Crisco lard was sitting on the green linoleum counter with a large bowl of dough beside it. Fry bread was in the making. He pointed to a worn green plastic chair at the kitchen table opposite him. "Sit, let me tell you about salt. There is a village of Creston, about twenty miles north of Natchitoches, or a mile north of Black Lake. North of Creston is a low place called Salt Lick. This is where the salt comes up and out of the ground. There are lots of mounds around this Salt Lick, extending from the highland on every side down to the slopes and even out on the low, flatland bordering the lick, where the ground is seldom dry or arid. There is another Salt Lick north of Shamrock on the Calvin Freeman farm. Many house mounds are on the south side of this lick going to the edge of the marsh southward."

Pointing a shaking finger, he pointed to the window, "Long ago, we were taught in school that a Mr. Freeman unearthed some skeletons when plowing deeper than customary during planting season. The bones were well preserved in the salt."

A teenage girl burst into the room, "Mom, when are we going to eat, I'm starving! Oh, Grandpa's telling stories again! He's always telling stories! He's crazy, you know? He has dementia. We learned about it in school. Mom, when are we going to eat?"

"Shhh! Show respect! Out with you, Out!" Bernadette swatted the teenager on the butt with her dishcloth. "I will call you when food is ready, now out!"

The teenager fled the kitchen. Attention was turned back to Grandpa. His face was white and his hands were shaking badly. "Douy-ya-shun-dah! She is filled with rage. It will hurt her." Shaking his head, he continued, "There was a time when the Elders spoke to one another and decided which Ways were to be told and which Ways were to be kept within moieties or clan families. This was one of those Ways taught to me and my brothers. My older sister was taken into the Story Holding clan, but that was long ago."

Bernadette moved to the dough on the counter, flattening it with a rolling pin into pie shaped pieces. Into a deep pan on the woodstove, she dropped the formed dough. The dough bubbled up crisp in the spitting hot Crisco lard, sizzling.

"This Old Salt Woman was a Way of reminding those of why it is important to be respectful. Respect is honor. When one is respectful of others, one has honor for oneself. There was a time when Honor became who a person was, what a person was remembered for and the most important message of a person's life." Shaking his head, he added, "Not any more. People hurt one another, they have no respect for themselves or others. There is no respect or honor."

A large plate with hot fry bread was placed in front of Grandpa. His whole face lit up, "Bernadette makes fry bread like my daughter did. Old Salt Woman did not have fry bread, which is sad."

Bernadette tilted the honey container over the Grandpa's fry bread. Grandpa greedily grabbed the honey coated delight, ripping large pieces to stuff into his mouth. He gummed the pieces with joy.

Then, no sooner was the last of his fry bread swallowed when he fell face first out of the wheelchair. Bernadette screamed. Everyone raced about in pandemonium. An ambulance was called. Within an hour a gurney appeared, oxygen, blood pressure cuff, cell phone calls that wouldn't go through, land-line phones with men in white coats frantically speaking with a doctor. The phone going back and forth from one medic to the other while one or the other worked on Grandpa.

Siren wailing, the ambulance disappeared down the four mile dirt drive to the main highway. Getting on I-40, the ambulance moved around Gallup onto Albuquerque. Family members piled into cars as teenagers were left to make their own fry bread. The race to save a life was in full movement. The hour and a half drive to the University of New Mexico Hospital ended with a quick turnaround to drive to the Indian Hospital in Gallup. Gallup had been passed an hour ago on the way to Albuquerque. Bernadette and her friend Sam firing off insults to the University of New Mexico Hospital in their native language of Keres as they drove hurriedly behind the ambulance.

As ambulance and cars neared the Gallup Hospital; two Bureau of Indian Police cars came as an escort. Seven people filled the waiting room of worn linoleum flooring and tired burgundy plastic chairs. Grandpa was admitted. He lived, barely. His heart was weak. His breathing erratic. His blood pressure dangerously high and in need of being monitored. Discussions took place, "He won't want to die in this death house. Sendo needs to be home. What do these nurses know about Sendo?"

The doctor was Anglo. He walked down the hall to the waiting room in his white physician's coat. His hair was white. His eyes were brown. "Are you here about your Grandfather?" Everyone nodded. He moved to sit next to Bernadette for she was the oldest in the room. "He is a strong man. Anyone else would have died in the ride across country. His heart is weak, but his spirit is strong."

Now he was speaking their language. "He will be here for a week to ten days. If his blood pressure can be stabilized, he can go back to Shi-wi. If his heart cannot handle being moved, he will be taken to the Hospice Center near Rehoboth. Would this be all right with you?"

Bernadette nodded. Sam kicked her foot. Keres conversation took place, more slowly this time. "We will need to take him home to the rez to die if he must die." Bernadette held her head high, her chin jutted out with her firm decision.

Four days. Four days later, the old man with the bad heart was home lying on a cot in the front room. The television was off. The room was crowded with family and friends, some had come from as far away as California. Searching the room for one person, he pointed. "You come here, the rest of you leave us. It is time I tell my story. Let me tell Old Salt Woman to a person who wants to hear the way of Old Salt Woman."

Four days. Four days later, Grandpa was too ill to speak. His story finished. The last two days, everyone was in the room, sitting quietly, listening to the soft voice of a powerful Way told from one generation to the next. It was two in the morning of the fifth day when everyone was awakened. A blanket was unrolled, an old man was carried outside in the peace of Night Sky to the flatland. It was time for them to sing his last song.

Mesa land was silhouetted in the dark skyline. A soft wind blew, scattering spirit prayers over the rabbit bush and chamisa. Juniper trees rattled dried berries as dwarfed pine trees danced with the breeze. Respect and honor. Respect and Honor were given this early morn with the dawning of Sun Father.

14 Grandfather's Old Salt Woman
(Pueblo and Lipan Apache)

She was white. All white. Her hair was in long braids with loose bangs flowing around her round face. She had a white buckskin manta dress. It was old, dirty on the ends. She never took her manta dress off her thin body. The buckskin dress, once glowing white, had fit her. Her dark skin set off the dirty whiteness of her dress. Some say she was the child of the Cloud People. The Cloud People placed Salt Woman on the earth to help them with their cooking and the keeping of their food in winter.

As a girl, Salt Woman was swayed and captured by a magical flute player. The flute player slid down the Milky Way to play his flute for Mother Earth's people. His music was to trick people into following him up into the sky place. When Salt Woman heard the music of the Flute Player, she found her heart was with him. For four nights and four days, the Flute Player blew his music across the earth. The Cloud People did not notice her with Flute Player. Many did not see her follow him to earth.

Cloud Mother, however, noticed her daughter as she followed Flute Player. Cloud Mother saw her daughter now with a rounder face, her eyes glowing with happiness, and her ankles swollen. Cloud Mother knew her daughter had been with a man, probably the Flute Player. Flute Player had noticed the beauty of Salt Woman. His affection for her was quick and sincere. Cloud Mother explained what had happened to the Cloud People Chief. He was furious. He sent down his men to collect Flute Player and bring him back to the Sky.

Salt Woman was left alone on earth with no music and a child on the way. The Cloud People told Cloud Mother that her daughter was now bound to the earth for she had broken the laws of the Cloud People. Cloud Mother cried for four days. For Four days the rain fell, thunder roared, and lightning was sent by Sky Father.

Soon Salt Woman, daughter of Cloud Mother and Sky Father gave birth to a weak, small boy. Whenever the boy tried to speak, music came out of his mouth. He could not eat without music coming from him. This boy grew slowly, weakly and without purpose. He was sad most times. Other times he whined a tune that grated on his mother's nerves. She did not leave him alone, but took his hand and had him follow her. This little boy was the opposite of Salt Woman. He was pale, with curly hair, had small eyes that teared all the time and was sullen for he was afraid of anyone and everyone.

Cloud Mother noticed animals followed Salt Woman and her small son. Animals would lick the earth near where they camped. Wherever Salt Woman walked a white dust fell from her legs. This powder was magical. Many times the powder saved an animal's life. All different animals and birds were loyal to Salt Woman. Often they protected her from the weather by showing her caves or where there was flowing water and how to be safe from flash floods. Salt Woman was kind to the animals as well. She never hurt them. Her son was too weak to hunt, he was too weak to leave her side.

Salt Woman dragged her son with her in search of Flute Player. Even as her body aged, her spirit remained young in its love for Flute Player. She went from Pueblo to Pueblo searching for him. Most of the pueblos would invite her to eat with them, although they were cautious of her whining small son. When Salt Woman would lift her manta to scrape the skin powder from inside her thighs into a bowl as exchange for the pueblo's kindness, the women of the pueblo were disgusted. Many times this caused the people to remove her from their feast before she or her son could eat anything. Mudheads were called, for they were the guardians of the people, to remove her. They would carry her to the edge of the Pueblo and dump her in the dirt. Her son would follow, crying.

Animals gave their lives to her so she and her son could eat and survive. This was great magic and Cloud Mother saw this and blessed the animals. Salt

Woman did not give up her search for Flute Player nor her yearning for him. Her small son would cry out in pain after walking a short distance. He was pathetic in his ability to keep with her, to understand her search. His clothes were ragged, muddy, and frayed. What a sad creature to be born from such magic and love.

At one point, during one of their walks, he ran away. The people found him, crying behind a woodshed. When they approached him, he screamed out a high note, piercing the air, frightening everyone. Putting their fingers in their ears, the strong men lifted him and returned him to his mother. The Northern Pueblo people did not want him for they did not want their children to be as he was.

Salt Woman continued on her quest for her Flute Player. Lifting her dress to scrape her powder from her thighs at Kapo Pueblo, the other women in the large kitchen scolded her for being disrespectful of the feast. The Mudheads were called. Confusion surrounded her as she tried to explain how the salt would help the taste of the food and would help in keeping it during the winter. Some women wanted her to explain further while others were screeching for the large Mudheads to remove her promptly.

In all of this chaos, her son ran away to hide. Salt Woman searched for him all through the cold of winter. No one would help her for no one wanted him found.

After his disappearance, her beautiful white buckskin dress or manta became torn and worn. Her hair became matted with leaves and her face wrinkled and dried. All through the times of blowing snow, the nights of quiet freeze and the days of overcast sleet, she searched for him. Animals came out at night to lead her into shelter, but at first light she was once again out, looking for any trace of him. For he was hers, the son of her love for the Flute Player.

No matter where she went, she was turned away from each of the Posoge'o'nwi'towa or Pueblo People's villages. Her filthy appearance, tragic loss and eagerness to find her son took her from Pueblo to Pueblo. At Kotyete feast day, she entered the pueblo from the east. The people knew she was a strong spirit, but she smelled and was filthy. No one wanted to invite her inside their house to share in their feast for no one wanted to have her near them. Salt Woman was desperately hungry and tired.

During a time of a hard rain, flash floods raced down the canyons, over cliffs and washed many of the Pueblo lands fields downstream into arroyos.

The people felt they had been cursed by the spirits, but no one understood why. Salt Woman took this time to move from the Rio Grande valley region to the east. At the Pueblo of Abo, the people came out to greet her. Her hair had been washed by the rain. Her manta was now white and her skin glowed as the sun shone through the clouds. Women invited her into their homes. They combed her hair, removing leaves and matted gnarls with burrs. The men brought the thinly sliced meat from outside to her. Everyone left her alone with the meat laid out on a flat stone outside of the cooking room. Salt Woman scraped her thigh into her hand. Once her hand was filled with the fine white powder, she sprinkled it over the slices of meat.

Once finished, she would walk out into the center of the Pueblo. Drums would softly beat, the chanters would sing for her and children brought her fresh bread and hot stew. Her days at Abo Pueblo were good. After finishing her task at Abo, others arrived. Women and men came from the northeast from the Pueblo of Kuah-aye. They brought her hand-drilled turquoise necklaces. Children took her hand to lead her to their Pueblo. Kuah-aye Pueblo had a fast flowing stream filled with trout. The people wanted the fish to be kept fresh and edible through the cold winters. Again, she was treated with great respect for the people knew she had a great gift to share.

After she had rested, been fed a fine meal, washed with her hair cleaned and combed, she was left alone with the thinly sliced fish. Kuah-aye had placed the fish, layer upon layer, on treated animal skins that were tied to poles. This elevated the fish off the ground, keeping it safe from vermin and varmints. Salt Woman once again, scraped her thighs, placing the white powder into bowls left beside the tied poles. Carefully, the powder was sprinkled over each piece of layered fish. This took her most of the day.

Soon her job at Kuah-aye was done. New people arrived from Quelooshe-aye Pueblo, which was further to the southwest. Walking with the people, this journey took several long days. Again, she was treated with great respect. Women washed her body carefully. Her manta was mended and washed. The younger women sang to her as they combed and braided her hair with bright flowers. Kuah-aye was near the plains. The hunters brought her stews filled with fresh meat while the grandmothers gave her fresh bread and roasted small corn.

Here Salt Woman rested. Children played around her. Dogs licked her feet and the woman told her stories of their families and cooking recipes. The summer passed pleasantly for Salt Woman. As fall approached, hunters took her to their skinning sheds. Salt Woman watched them hang, clean and slice the meat. As they were ready to roll the meat for winter, she stopped them. Telling them how to cure meat, she asked them to leave her. Taking large round black bowls from the side of the sheds, she scraped her thighs, filling each bowl full of white salt.

Calling the men back into the sheds, she showed them how to cure the meat. They watched as she put the salt on the flat meat. Then she took a stone and beat the salt into the meat, turning it as she did so. Each side was salted, pounded and then the meat was rolled tightly to be hung from the rafters of each shed. She taught the men to do this and she watched, making sure it was done correctly. Everyone appreciated her gift, her knowledge and her kindness.

When the fall winds began to blow across the flatland, Salt Woman told the people it was time for her to go. The people offered her food to take, but she chose to go only with their kind appreciation. Walking into the wind, she moved to the northeast. There she arrived at a low lying lake. The water was still and smelled putrid. Salt Woman found a small mound to dig shelter. As night fell, wild dogs circled around her. She clapped her hands, flinging salt out into the spoiled water. In the morning, the water had dark substances bubbling up in between the floating blocks of powdered salt.

Here at this strange white pond of black floating muck, she fasted for four days, praying with all her might for the return of the Flute Player and her son. Tears from her sadness filled the long canyon to make a large lake of salt. Animals came to her bringing her food for survival. Cloud Mother watched her daughter and sent rain to her for clean drinking water.

On the fifth morning, Salt Woman said goodbye to her animal friends and moved west to Ten-abo. There was no one there. All she found was an empty pueblo ruin. Hawks and ravens guided her to the west where she arrived at Tey-pan-ya. The people had heard of her with mixed reviews. Some knew she was gifted, but were unsure as to what her gift was. Others had been told she was a filthy woman who should not be allowed into the home. Her entrance was not wanted.

Walking further west, Salt Woman came to Pilabo. This was a small Pueblo populated mostly of the elderly. One grandmother gave Salt Woman a finely woven blanket to keep her warm in the cold winds. Kawaik Pueblo came into view as Salt Woman found herself hungry and tired. The women came to welcome her, but the men were not eager for her to stay. Older women told her of the illness that had come with the Apache raids. Some of the men felt Salt Woman was a bad omen of winter's death. Salt Woman stayed with an elderly grandmother at Kawaik for ten days, waiting for the weather to warm and the winds to cease. Finally, the Elders came to her and asked if she would please leave.

Wrapped in the blanket, Salt Woman walked in the cold snow to the base of Katz-i-moh Pueblo. Her fingers raw from the cold air and her feet cut from the sharp rocks, she worked her way up the steep path to the top of the mesa where the Pueblo sat. Men met her as she climbed into the south entry. They had their arms crossed with bows hanging on their shoulders, quivers filled with arrows slung across their backs. She didn't stop to speak with them, but shoved them aside to walk into the first house. There she pushed back the door-holding-blanket to enter the warmth of the big room.

Women scurried away from her with their children in front of them. Salt Woman sat in front of the roaring fire and relaxed. Soon after an Elder entered the big room. He sat beside her, quietly studying her. She ignored him. Finally, he asked, "Are you the woman who has the power to protect the meat during the winter?"

Salt Woman nodded. He continued to ask, "Are you the woman who shows the hunters how to keep their meat safe from disease?"

Salt Woman nodded. Again, he asked, "Are you the woman who is made of the white power that makes stews taste better?"

Salt Woman laughed, "How bad do your stews taste?" He laughed with her. A woman appeared from a side room carrying a pot of stew. She placed it on the large fire, stirring it occasionally. The Elder nodded to Salt Woman. Ladling some stew into a small bowl, he gave this to Salt Woman with a chunk of freshly baked bread. Dipping the chunk of bread into the stew, she tasted it. "Yes, I can help this stew taste better, but you need to leave the room."

Katz-i-moh Pueblo asked her to stay until the coldest winds ceased. The women brought her their winter stews and alone she helped with the taste. Feast days were filled with laughter and warmth by large fires as the people appreciated her. Stories were traded and food was salted and then the sun returned and the wind went north. Again, it was time for Salt Woman to move. The children escorted her down the steep mesa path to the flatland. The people watched her move west to Aco-ma.

The people of Aco-ma were cautious of outsiders for they had survived a horrible drought, illness and a time when all the dead and down firewood around them had been soaked by dry rain. The people believed a Bad Spirit was coming. Salt Woman was not welcome and she was not trusted. Men met her at the base of Aco-ma with spears. She had no need of speaking with them, but continued west. Entering Na'nizhoozhi, Salt Woman hurried into the tall home in the center. There she found a group of women waiting for her. The fire pit was roaring with dried pinion wood, the smell was welcoming and the food placed around the pit inviting. The women hurriedly took her wet blanket to place on the stone floor to dry. They brought her four large black bowls. After welcoming her, drying her hair and her feet, they departed the room.

Exhausted, but eager to please these women, Salt Woman scraped her thighs to fill all four of the large black bowls. Then she clapped her hands. The women returned to bring her wooden plates of hot food. Salt woman slept for five days and four nights. The people let her quietly rest as they fed the large fire pit with fresh wood to keep her warm. As the winter solstice came, the people invited her to share in the feast, the dances and the celebration of winter's end and the new life of the coming new sun.

Women came from neighboring Pueblos with empty bowls for her to fill. Men sat with her to learn how to prepare the meat for winter and for long hunting seasons. Children at her feet listened to her stories of animals and birds that had helped her. The people were grateful to her with hope that she would stay. As the cold winter moved to a warmer spring, Salt Woman took her blanket to continue her journey to the west.

Nakai-bit-oh was sheltered by the high canyon walls on the north side. Salt Woman was met by hungry women whose men had gone off to hunt in the winter and had not returned. As much as they needed help, Salt Woman knew of her goal. She must reach Ah-shi-wi-wi before the heat of the season of high sun. Hurrying on her way, she arrived at Ah-shi-wi-wi on the fourth day of spring planting on top of the mesas. The women were pleased to have her stay with them. The men were not sure of her for she arrived dirty, thin, and haggard now bent with age.

Salt Woman was now tired from her sadness and her confusion of people. Again, the women asked her for salt, which she gave to them freely. The men asked her advice and this was given. Children held her hands only to be pleased when once they let go, they licked their fingers. As the morning sun lifted on the fifth morning of her stay at Ah-shi-wi-wi, Salt Woman walked away from another Pueblo.

At Halona-Wi, where the canyons fall away to flatland and the sky greets the earth is a lake. Lifting her hands to the clouds overhead, Salt Woman calmly walked into the lake. As her body entered, the water turned white with the powder from her body. Birds flew around her, coyotes howled as the Water Spirit took her into its arms. She is at peace. Salt Woman in her lake demands respect and one must have honor to retrieve the salt or there is none to find. This is the Way of Salt Woman or Mowa Senda. There is no more to say for now you know more than the teller of this story.

15 Story of Nalq (Tsimshian)

There was a place near a river far to the north where time was not important. One night, older children were playing outside for the sun stayed longer when night began to fall. The older children were pushing, laughing and not listening to their parents who were having a meeting in a community hut. One of the older boys, pointed to the sky. There descending, straight at them was a magnificent feather. The feather was long and wispy with the colors of deepest night, purple black with hidden silver streaks.

The older boy jumped to catch the tip of the feather. His hold on it was tight, he pulled with all his might. As he began to fall to the ground, his hands became stuck fast to the feather. Slowly, ever so slowly, the feather ascended. Barely pulling the boy with it for the others noticed his entrapment. Another tall boy grabbed his friend's feet to weigh him down. His hands stuck fast to his friend's feet. Screaming for help, others jumped to grab his ankles and feet. They too were stuck fast.

Gently, gently the magnificent feather rose in the night, slowly, slowly pulling a long chain of older children with it. Parents turned in the meeting to hear their children screaming. Racing outside, they grabbed at the feet of their offspring. Again, hands stuck to feet. Grandparents were attached, younger children became part of this ascending population. All of the village rose into the sky that night, except for one young woman and her new born infant.

Being dark and cold, people were lifted high into the night sky. In a blink, the long magnificent feather evaporated into a thousand stars. Bodies plummeted to the earth, crashing, smashing into pieces, dying on the midnight plain they were no more. The young woman, daughter of the chief of the village, came outside to find her family, friends and fellow villagers dead. She wept and wept in heavy sorrow.

While she wept deeply in her pain, she wiped her nose on her sleeve to fling the mucous onto the ground. As the mucous hit the earth, a baby boy appeared. Knowing this was great magic, she quickly found a grindstone to put next to her body. Breaking off a branch from a crabapple tree, she placed it next to her left bosom heavy with milk. Taking a shell from the shelf, she put this next to her right bosom. Between her two breasts was placed a long raven feather. Gathering the baby boy into her arms, she wrapped him in brown fur of a marten. Once inside her hut, she washed his face with her tears.

Lying down with him on her palate, she removed the grindstone from her body. Putting the grindstone down on the thick bear blanket, it became a baby boy. His face was washed with her tears as she wrapped him in a sea-otter blanket. Removing the raven feather from between her breasts, she placed this on the furry blanket. As her tears touched the feather, it became a baby boy. Removing the shell from her other breast, placing it on the fur blanket, this became a baby girl. Again, the crabapple tree branch was placed beside these two and became another baby boy. She gave names to her children. The first one she called Nalq or Mucous. This was to be the gift of the oldest child. The second one she named Little Grindstone. The third one was Little Shell and then there was Little Crabapple and Little Feather, the last one was called Knife in Hand.

These children grew quickly. Their mother watched over them, teaching them the ways of the old village. One day, the children wandered far from home to come to a large plain. There they found human bones all over the ground. The bones were large and small having fallen from the sky, they were all about the land. When they returned home, they asked their mother about the human bones.

Holding her children close to her, she told them, "There was a time when the children were outside playing at night. They were making too much noise and the Sky Chief was disturbed by their loud playing. He sent down a long magnificent feather. A tall powerful child grabbed hold of the feather and all the other people in the village grabbed hold to pull him back to earth, but the feather kept lifting them higher and higher. When the Sky Chief was pleased with the quiet, he took the feather to let the people fall to their death on the ground."

Trying not to cry, she continued, "It is ever so important that when you play outside at night, be quiet. Don't play out on the open ground. Stay close to me and do not reach for a long feather if it comes down from the sky. Promise me this?"

The children hugged her, saying, "We will be careful and we won't grab onto a long feather."

Unfortunately, she believed them. Time passed, as it does, and the children were outside of the village playing in the early night. They were shouting, laughing and roughing around in their fun. A long magnificent feather descended down from the dark sky. The children studied it with amazement. Little Feather wrapped his hands around the tip of the feather as it slowly, slowly lifted him. Mucous realized Little Feather was being lifted, he grabbed his feet. Little Grindstone raced to hold onto Mucous. Little Crabtree reached out his long arms to become branches, holding onto Little Grindstone's legs. Little Crabtree turned into a tree with deep roots sunk into the ground. The feather continued to lift, ripping the tree roots from the ground.

Knife Hand sharpened her hand. Climbing up the Crabapple tree, Little Grindstone to Mucous and finally to the top of Little Feather's head, she cut the end off of the feather. Falling free, the children hit the ground hard, smashing their bodies into pieces. Knife Hand gasped as she held fast to Little Feather's hair, swinging the knife over her brothers' bodies, they slowly, slowly came back to life. Little Feather held fast to the tip of the magnificent feather. Now, they remembered the story their mother had told them. Realizing the power of the feather and the power of their sister's knife, they went to the place of human bones.

Taking the bones and putting them together as best they could, their sister waved her magic knife over them. Some men's heads were put on women's bodies. Some women's bodies were fixed with children's heads. All the bones were mixed on each body. Today, we have some bodies that are small with large heads and men's heads on women's bodies. Working quickly, the children were eager to please their mother and they did the best they could with their young knowledge. Many had broken bones and were in extreme pain until Little Feather waved the tip of the magnificent feather over them to have the bones quickly heal. This was very magical.

Once home, they explained to their mother about their mishap and the magic they performed. Flying into a rage, she shook her children to say, "You never should have touched that feather! You took part of the feather! The Sky Chief will hunt you down for destroying his magic! This is bad! This is wrong!"

Little Feather explained, "Mother, we brought your village back to life. Come and see. The people you loved and your friends are here, come and see!"

Walking out to the strange group of people standing in front of her hut, the mother cried, "This is wrong! What have you done! This is wrong, these people died and should be honored, not made into unfortunates!" Whirling around, she pointed her finger, "Get out! Get out of this village! Get out, be gone! You are no longer my children!"

Turning from her, the four boys and one girl walked out of the village. They walked for several days not speaking. Soon, they came upon a blind man holding a finely woven net. He was sitting on a flat stone near the top of a mountain. Mucous went to the net, he touched it saying, "This will tell us what he has in his net."

Suddenly, the man said, "I have lost mucous, I have lost mucous!"

They laughed at him to continue on their journey. On their path they found a raccoon with a piece of wood stuck between its teeth. The Raccoon was unable to remove the wood. Little Grindstone took a piece of stone to strike Raccoon on the head and killed him. They removed the wood from Raccoon's mouth and went on their way. Smelling delicious food, they found a hut with a grandmother inside cooking.

She invited them into her home. Stirring her pot, she asked them of their journey. They told her of their meeting the blind man with a net. Grandmother asked them if they had seen Grandfather while coming to her. They told her of Raccoon with a piece of wood in its mouth. Grindstone said, "We killed him and removed the wood. He is still dead on the path." Laughing, he smiled at her.

Shrieking in pain, Grandmother called out, "Windows close, doors close, fire burn, smoke hole close!" She disappeared up the chimney before the smoke hole began to shut. Little Feather turned into a bird to fly quickly through the smoke hole as it shut tight. The others were left inside, coughing, crying and begging to be let out before they died.

Little Feather hurried to the place where dead Raccoon lay. Waving his feather over Raccoon, he came back to life. Raccoon asked him to gather wood. The three others were dying in the hut. As soon as their arms were filled with dried wood, they went back to the hut. Raccoon called out, "Grandmother, open the door and let me inside!"

As soon as Grandmother heard Grandfather's voice, she said, "Come inside! Open the doors! Open the windows! Open the smoke hole!" Smoke poured out of the hut, rising quickly in the air. Little Feather went into the hut, waving the tip of the magnificent feather, he brought his brothers and sister back to life. They continued on their journey.

Their mother stayed in the village with her strange friends. She nurtured many, nursed some of them into better health and some she taught how to be human again. Her magic is good and her love is remembered. Her children, however, continued on their path of destruction and learning. Eventually, they grew wise as is the way with all children. These children became: Crabapple Tree, Little Feather, Little Grindstone, Knife Hand and Mucous. It is said Knife Hand had ten children, nine boys and one girl. The youngest one had a blue hole in his left cheek. We can only pray our children learn from their parents' mistakes.

www.ingramcontent.com/pod-product-compliance
Lightning Source LLC
Chambersburg PA
CBHW031147090426
42738CB00008B/1258